WITHDRAWN

D1248535

ON RESEARCH LIBRARIES

THE M.I.T. PRESS
Massachusetts Institute of Technology
Cambridge, Massachusetts, and London, England

American Council of Learned Societies Devoted to Humanistic Studies.

On Research Libraries

Statement and Recommendations of the Committee on Research Libraries of the American Council of Learned Societies

Submitted to

National Advisory Commission on Libraries

November 1967

Set in Caledonia and printed and bound
in the United States of America by
Rose Printing Company, Inc.

Library of Congress catalog card number: 73–83404

Foreword

This is the formal report of the Committee on Research Libraries appointed and sponsored by the American Council of Learned Societies. The ACLS Committee was created in response to a request from the National Advisory Commission on Libraries for a study of research libraries and recommendations for their future development.

The ACLS undertook this study with alacrity in view of its enduring commitment to the effective performance of the nation's research libraries and its knowledge of the manifold problems with which they are now beset.

At its first meeting on March 2, 1967, the Committee drew up a plan of inquiry and assigned responsibility for each major topic to two or three of its members. Papers were then commissioned and as they were written provided a basis for discussion at succeeding meetings attended by their authors. The Committee's report was then drawn from the minutes of the meetings and the papers, several of which are incorporated in it.

On behalf of the ACLS I wish to thank the authors of the commissioned papers and the librarians, scholars, and university administrators who made up the Committee, and who jointly with the authors generated and shaped the Statement and Recommendations which follow.

I am satisfied that the Committee's findings and proposals deserve the most thoughtful study and evaluation—not only by the National Commission but by everyone who is concerned with the ability of our libraries to facilitate scholarship and inquiry.

I wish also to thank the Council on Library Resources, and particularly Verner W. Clapp, who was then its President, for the grant which made the study possible.

Frederick Burkhardt
President
American Council of Learned Societies

Committee on Research Libraries

CHAIRMAN: *Frederick Burkhardt*
President
American Council of Learned Societies

William O. Baker
Vice President-Research
Bell Telephone Laboratories

Kingman Brewster, Jr.
President
Yale University

T. Robert S. Broughton
Paddison Professor of Classics
University of North Carolina

Douglas W. Bryant
University Librarian
Harvard University

Lyman H. Butterfield
Editor-in-Chief, *The Adams Papers*
Massachusetts Historical Society

William S. Dix
Librarian of the University
Princeton University

Herman H. Fussler
Director of the Library
University of Chicago

Warren J. Haas
Director of Libraries
University of Pennsylvania

Chauncy D. Harris
Professor of Geography
University of Chicago

James D. Hart
Professor of English
University of California, Berkeley

Committee's Preface

We welcome this opportunity to direct attention to the critical needs of American research libraries and to recommend measures which in our judgment would enable them to make their full contribution to the achievement of our national objectives now and in the future.

Since World War II the nation's research libraries have responded with energy and imagination to the widening interests of scholarship in the humanities, the social sciences, the natural sciences, and the professions, to the requirements of new and expanding universities, and to the urgent informational demands of government and industry.

In recent years, however, we have been deeply concerned by the mounting evidence that these libraries are facing serious difficulties which will, if not relieved, critically impair their performance. Shortages of space, staff, and funds are only the more obvious consequences of the double challenge of the greatly increased demand for their services and an unprecedented increase in publication at home and abroad.

We offer no panaceas for the problems of the research libraries, but we have no doubt that they can be largely overcome by a carefully designed combination of measures including a substantial admixture of research and development.

It is a major finding of our Committee that whatever measures of self-help the libraries take, individually and cooperatively, there can be no steady progress toward a coherent national library system without major Federal participation in leadership and support. Given the Federal library structure we propose, and the continuing interest and concern of the Administration, the Congress, and other agencies, we are confident that the nation's research libraries will be able to respond much more effectively to the increasingly critical needs of our society.

In presenting our report to the National Advisory Commission on Libraries, we cannot claim full agreement on the phrasing of any particular recommendation or its rationale or its relative importance in the list. However, we are in substantial agreement on the content and purport of our Statement and Recommendations. We address them not only to the Commission, the Administration, and the Congress but to everyone concerned with the library's contribution to the quality of inquiry, policy, and scholarship.

ACLS Committee on Research Libraries

Introduction

If the peculiar trait of man among living creatures is his capacity for thought, the peculiar mark of civilized man is his habit of recording knowledge for communication to other men, whether near or far in place or in time. For this purpose he has invented and used a vast variety of instruments and materials, from clay, papyrus, ink, paper, and the printing press to phonodiscs, magnetic tapes bearing symbols rather than letters and words, and photochromic dyes that can fix thousands of miniaturized characters on a chip of film an inch or two square. But in whatever form individual men have chosen to put down their thoughts and observations, they have for a very long time now taken pains to put them in safe places to which other men, before and afterward, have committed theirs.

From the time we know anything of history, such accumulations, known as archives and libraries, have enjoyed a kind of sanctity as embodying the best efforts of men's minds. A barbarian was one who would or did destroy records of gathered knowledge in an enemy's country. Thus the library, as it has evolved in the Western world from the archival rooms of palaces in old Mediterranean lands, has become the symbol as well as the actual center of men's aspiration to better themselves and their society.

This is nowhere more strikingly true than in the United States. In its colonial era America inherited the ideas of Western Europe through the migration here of books as well as people. Since its birth as a nation it has helped reshape and give the best of those ideas substance by its commitment to the proposition that intellectual freedom is an essential ingredient of political freedom—or, as Jefferson put it, that error is dangerous only when we are not free to contradict it. Economic developments in the nineteenth century and political events in the twentieth have broadened and deepened this trend. The growing wealth of the United States, together with its comparative security from wars that have ravaged most other parts of the world, has brought more and more treasures for safekeeping to our libraries, provided training and facilities for several generations of American scholars who now match in eminence their counterparts in older centers of learning, and attracted to this country increasing numbers of experts in all fields of thought and investigation.

These developments and others familiar enough in the life of our time have placed libraries at the heart of most of the worthy enterprises that Americans conduct. They are an indispensable part of our enormous educational effort on all its levels. American business and industry today support thousands of specialized libraries because they are vital to their operations and progress; the quality of its library resources and services is a reliable index to the quality of many types of corporations. Modern science, which is rendering so much of the world obsolete so fast and which is profoundly impatient with libraries as men have customarily built and operated them, is just as profoundly dependent on them for access to and dissemination of the data and findings it feeds on.

Finally, government itself is one of the chief consumers, as it is one of the chief producers, of library goods and one of the chief operators of library services. In 1814, when Jefferson offered his library to the nation at a nominal price after the burning of the infant Library of Congress, some Congressmen doubted the wisdom of purchasing such a collection. What need could officers of the United States have, they asked, for books written in foreign languages, including Greek, Latin, and Anglo-Saxon? Today, under the authority of recent legislation, the Library of Congress endeavors to acquire a copy of every book of substantial value published in *any* language. All of this is not only natural and proper but represents a trend that will grow stronger rather than decline—always provided that human wisdom succeeds in preserving human civilization.

The worth and importance of libraries in general, then, may

be taken as virtually self-evident. We are concerned here, however, with one type of library, the research library, and the adequacy of its performance as the rising demands for its services coincide with a tidal wave of new publication the world over. The collections and services of the nation's research libraries undergird the whole library structure as well as higher education and scholarship in every area of human significance.

Research libraries may be defined as institutions whose collections are organized primarily to meet the needs of scholars and so to facilitate effective action on the frontier of every field of knowledge, traditional and novel. Most American research libraries are integral parts of universities. At their best they are notable for the variety and depth of their holdings and for the quality of research that they support. The collections of the seventy university libraries that are members of the Association of Research Libraries range in size from half a million to almost eight million volumes. The present average is just over a million and a half; it will approach three million in less than twenty years.

These relatively well-stocked libraries make an indispensable contribution to higher education and research in every section of the country. Increasingly their collections are used by scholars from all parts of the world; each year their lending to other libraries and photocopying for research mount; and steadily their role in higher education expands as the universities to which they belong account for eighty percent of the nation's doctorates. Any inadequacy in the range or depth of their research materials or their services will jeopardize American scholarship and limit its services both to ourselves and to the world. At the same time the extraordinary needs of the numerous new or expanding universities should be given earnest attention. Their research collections must be built up almost over night if they are to attract able faculty, offer graduate work worthy of the name, and contribute adequately to their communities, states, and regions.

In addition to university libraries the Association of Research Libraries includes three Federal Libraries, one of which—the Library of Congress—holds some of the world's greatest research collections; two public libraries with important resources for research; and several unaffiliated libraries. Outside the Association are institutions of the first rank, such as the Folger Shakespeare Library and the American Antiquarian Society, distinguished by priceless materials in history, literature, and other fields that are vital to scholarship and placed freely at its service. These unaffiliated libraries have no alumni, and where they lack adequate endowment, their very existence may be threatened as expenses rise. Yet if the premise is granted that the nation's resources for promoting knowledge are indivisible, it should be clear that no part of its network of research libraries can be impaired without impairing all.

PROBLEMS OF RESEARCH LIBRARIES

While there is diversity in the age, size, control, and clientele of American research libraries, they are all faced with refractory problems that impede their satisfactory performance. At first glance the dilemma of the research library appears to be simply the consequence of growth. It is axiomatic that American research libraries double in size every fifteen to twenty years and it follows that they must be chronically short of space, staff, and funds. But just as challenging as these shortages are the accelerating demands that have been made upon American research libraries since World War II. Their services have been heavily taxed by the rising university population, a fourfold growth in graduate enrollment, and a sharp increase in postdoctoral research. The demand for information from the business and industrial world has multiplied, and the government's massive investment in research and development has added substantially to library burdens without compensatory support. Even foundation grants for research, welcome as they are, have further taxed library resources without proportionate financial relief. At the same time the national interest has necessitated knowledge of cultures and geographical areas we previously ignored; and the widened angle of vision of American scholarship, as well as of education, industry and government, has obliged libraries to seek out and acquire research materials in countries without bibliographical tools or a book trade and in languages totally unknown to their own catalogers.

These new demands and developments have called into question the research library's habitual pattern of acquisition and cataloging. When American scholarship staked out the whole world as its sphere of interest, it was no longer possible for research libraries to do all their foreign buying through a few reputable dealers in Western Europe; and when an Asian and African inflow began through other channels, much of it defied the skills of the local catalogers. Arrearages in cataloging mounted also at the Library of Congress with serious consequences for other libraries. From the first of the century it had shared its cataloging skills with other libraries by selling them catalog cards, but in recent years it has been able to supply cards to other research libraries for no more than half of their foreign purchases. This has meant wasteful duplication of effort on a large scale and intense competition for a limited number of specialized catalogers. At many libraries research materials piled up that could not be cataloged or even fully identified, and to this degree the librarian was no longer in bibliographical control.

At the same time the proliferation of publication here and abroad raised serious questions about the adequacy of the bibliographical apparatus on which scholars depend for notice of everything published that may be relevant to their research. What bibliographical information they received on current research materials, whether American or foreign, was frequently out-of-date, and they were supplied with virtually no information about foreign books or periodicals that were not bought and cataloged by an American library.

While the librarian was adding more volumes to his collections than ever before, he was becoming increasingly aware of the impermanence of a substantial proportion of his institution's past acquisitions. Older books were surviving well, but most works published during the last hundred years were printed on paper whose acid content would bring about its disintegration in a matter of decades. In consequence, research libraries had to divert part of their budgets to photocopying books whose pages were too fragile for further use. And since there has been no general move to adopt acid-free papers on the part of the Government Printing Office or commercial publishers, the cost of photocopying is likely to rise on a curve that parallels the graph of acquisitions a generation earlier.

Research libraries could have faced these challenging developments with greater assurance had they been adequately staffed, but the demand for American librarians at home and abroad outstripped supply in the 1950's, and libraries of all types were henceforth understaffed, with persistent vacancies at every level of skill and authority. Research libraries had special staffing difficulties because their requirements for linguistic and subject-matter competence go far beyond standard library training, and catalogers were in especially short supply. The competitive bidding resulting from heightened demand has raised salary scales, but this and other persuasions to recruitment have not yet sufficed to interest as many able young men and women as are needed in library careers.

During these two decades, moreover, library costs were rising much more rapidly than the general price index, and in university budgets library needs were habitually underestimated. The financial needs of libraries are formidable today, and they are sure to become more formidable. Indeed, substantial new sources of income will have to be found if the nation's research libraries are to continue to perform their function satisfactorily. Libraries at new branches of state universities are immediately faced with the double cost of simultaneously acquiring retrospective and current material, and even established university libraries are confronted with sharply rising expenditures. According to a careful analysis and forecast, library costs at Harvard are expected to rise from $5,700,000 in 1964–1965 to $14,700,000 in 1975–76.[1]

To these developments must be added another which is at once a problem and a promise. This is the automation of the library's operational and bibliographical functions. Its promise is so clear that it is already being widely applied to the manifold routine tasks that libraries have hitherto had to perform manually. At the same time encouraging experiments are being conducted in coding catalog data for central storage, fast access, and mechanical transmission to a geographically unlimited constituency. How satisfactorily the intellectual content of books, manuscripts, and other library materials, as distinct from bibliographical description and indexing of them, can be coded for these purposes is currently unknown and a matter of debate. One daily hears and reads predictions of a breakthrough to a new world of electronic ease for librarians and scholars. Such predictions are delusive, and by their false promise impede more than they help those working toward solutions of research library problems by means within, just beyond, or even well beyond our grasp. As far ahead as can be foreseen, the computer and its accompaniments will supplement rather than replace the library materials we are familiar with, and even the most sophisticated electronic circuitry will remain an aid to, not a substitute for, men's minds in contact with books. But if wisdom cannot be extracted from machines, they are marvelously rapid and accurate processors and disseminators of information. They must therefore be developed to their fullest capacity in research libraries. Ambitious experiments are now in progress, and as more cost studies and performance reports become available, there is every prospect of steady and productive advance in this area.

Briefly stated, these are the major problems that face research libraries today, and vast resources of money and manpower, to say nothing of imagination, planning, and coopera-

[1] *The Harvard University Library, 1966–1976, Report of a Planning Study*, Cambridge, 1966, p. 29.

tion, will be required to resolve them. The future of our free society depends on our access to accumulated knowledge organized to facilitate learning and scholarship. Libraries are not inert repositories, of artifacts and documents of the past, or mere bits and pieces of information. They are living agencies for intellectual enrichment and progress, for public policy and social improvement through scholarship. They are at once man's memory and the embodiment of his faith that, despite the tragic vicissitudes of our time, his creations, his ideas, and his spirit will live forever.

There is a final problem for which neither this Committee nor presumably the National Advisory Commission on Libraries can offer a solution. "You have the ages for your guide," Edwin Arlington Robinson once told Americans, "but not the wisdom to be led." Libraries store wisdom, but they offer no guarantee that it will be effectively employed. Nevertheless, we can at least promise that, if the recommendations which follow are implemented, the United States in its research libraries will possess vastly more knowledge in a far more usable form than has been available to any other country in mankind's history.

Contents

Foreword *Frederick Burkhardt*		v
Members of the ACLS Committee on Research Libraries		vii
Committee's Preface		ix
Introduction		xi
Problems of Research Libraries		xiv
I.	Committee Recommendations	1
II.	Bibliographical Control and Physical Dissemination, *Edwin E. Williams*	26
	Bibliography in General	28
	Library Cataloging	32
	Collecting and Collections	39
	Coordination and Sharing of Resources	49
	General Observations	54
	Recapitulation	57
III.	Research Libraries and the New Technology *Max V. Mathews and W. Stanley Brown*	59
	Computer Technology	60
	Microform and Copying Technology	66
	Interactions between Libraries and Special-Purpose Libraries	70
	Recommendations	72
	Appendix: Costs Associated with the Machine-Readable Catalog	75
IV.	Research Libraries and the Federal Government *Charles Blitzer and Reuben Clark*	77
Appendix:	Copyright Problems of Research Libraries, *Ralph S. Brown, Jr.*	86
Selected References		100
Index		101

I

Committee Recommendations

Our research libraries are now confronted by serious problems that threaten the quality of their service to the nation. There is a growing realization that if these libraries were unable to function effectively the frontiers of knowledge would cease to advance, our understanding of the foreign world would lose its currency and its relevance to policy, and higher education would sink into mediocrity.

What those who do the nation's research need from our libraries can be simply stated: more informative, up-to-date, and efficient bibliographical services relating to books, manuscripts, official documents, pamphlets, and journals; and the ready availability across the nation of these and all other materials of value to research, including those relating to hitherto neglected foreign areas.

Our recommendations are designed to enable the nation's research libraries to meet these requirements so that our national purpose can be pursued with effectiveness and wisdom.

Underlying our recommendations is the firm conviction that these requirements can indeed be met if we clearly formulate our national goals and policy, coordinate the efforts that are now isolated, augment and organize our resources for optimum use, and obtain substantially more support of research libraries from both public and private sources. Furthermore, we are convinced that the measures that must be taken today need not foreclose tomorrow's options but should facilitate the realization of a coherent national system which makes use of modern technology whenever research will thereby be better served.

We assume that individual libraries will continue to do everything in their power to cope with their problems. The solution of staffing inadequacies, for example, will require study, planning, and Federal support; but the individual research library may be able to increase the effectiveness of its staff by such measures as job analysis, in-service training programs, the automation of library operations, and leaves of absence for summer institutes and graduate study.

We anticipate also that research libraries will continue to cooperate in a variety of projects and systems designed to enhance their utility to scholars. The research libraries of the United States have had an impressive record of achievement in such cooperative enterprises and programs as the National Union Catalog, the Farmington Plan, and innumerable research projects initiated and carried out by the Association of Research Libraries.

But whatever the libraries do for themselves, singly or in combination, it is a major finding of the ACLS Committee that the nation's research libraries cannot respond effectively to the ever-mounting demands made upon them by government, business, industry, and education without greater assistance and support from government and from the private sector. In particular, a coherent national system cannot be achieved without active Federal participation and support. For this reason we begin and end with recommendations which emphasize the crucial role that the Federal government must play in the evolving nationwide system of research libraries. It is clear, however, that Federal support alone cannot solve the problems of the libraries. The attainment of our objectives will require the intelligent, wholehearted, and sustained efforts of everyone concerned. We can pledge such efforts on the part of the universities, the scholarly societies, and the librarians.

A NATIONAL COMMISSION ON LIBRARIES

1. We recommend that a National Commission on Libraries and Archives be appointed by the President to serve on a continuing basis and to be responsible for Federal policy and programs relating to the nation's library, archival, and informational needs.[2]

The need for a National Commission on Libraries and Archives with adequate staff and authority has become increasingly apparent in recent years. Though concerned with all types and levels of library services, the Commission we propose would recognize that research libraries undergird all libraries and that their effective functioning is essential to the advancement of knowledge in all fields and to the quality of education. The Commission would therefore assist research libraries to develop their resources and facilities; to examine, adapt, and utilize the relevant applications of modern technology; to devise a system for increasing access to research materials throughout the nation; and to establish symbiotic relationships with research libraries overseas.

Where such a Library Commission should be located in the Federal organization is a question the President and Congress will decide. However, we consider it appropriate to place the Commission in the Department of Health, Education, and Welfare, directly under the Secretary, but reporting to the President and the Congress as well as to the Secretary. We conceive the main requirement to be that the Commission have authority to advise the Federal government on national needs in library services and development, on financial support, and on planning in the direction of a national library system.

It may be desirable also to establish a division of research library services in the Office of Education, possibly in the Bureau of Higher Education, to bring together certain Federal operations relating to research libraries, including the funding of direct support, construction, training, and research, to be carried out within policy guidelines laid down by the National Commission. If this is done the great research li-

[2] See Charles Blitzer and Reuben Clark, "Research Libraries and the Federal Government," pp. 77–85, *infra*.

braries and archival collections outside of the universities should be given the same standing and consideration as the university libraries.

Appointed by the President with the advice and consent of the Senate, the Library Commission should be representative of scholarship in all fields, the public interest, and the library profession. It should of course have a staff adequate to the performance of its functions. Such a Commission will in our view satisfy the manifold needs that owe their origin and present urgency to the lack of a central body with responsibility and authority to formulate a national library policy and to assure the effective performance of all libraries in the public interest.

ACQUISITION

2. We recommend that the National Commission on Libraries be given responsibility for policy and planning relating to the acquisition of research materials for the nation's libraries.

In fulfilling its responsibilities, the National Commission on Libraries and Archives must devote particular attention to the urgent problems relating to the acquisition of research materials wherever published, as well as to their cataloging, indexing, abstracting, preservation, and accessibility.

In each of these areas the National Commission should make recommendations for action to the appropriate operating agencies after it has surveyed the nation's needs, established priorities, formulated plans, and determined the most effective allocation of resources and responsibilities. The Commission should also maintain general supervision over the operating agencies, and should have a continuing role in informing the public and particularly the Congress on library needs and how they can be met in the interest of research. We take for granted that the Commission will make full use of the capabilities of the Library of Congress (whose expanded role as the national library is outlined in Recommendation 5), the National Library of Medicine, the National Agricultural Library, the Center for Research Libraries (see Recommendation 6), and other public and private institutions and organizations.

In the area of acquisition, the Commission will undoubtedly recognize the primacy of the Library of Congress among the nation's research libraries. Treaties and informal arrangements bring it a steady flow of official publications from abroad, and it is engaged in worldwide acquisition through two remarkable programs of great importance to research. One is known as the Public Law 480 Program. The other comes from Title II–C of the Higher Education Act of 1965 which authorizes appropriations to the Office of Education for transfer to the Library of Congress for the purpose of "acquiring, so far as possible, all library materials currently published throughout the world which are of value to scholarship."

In order that acquisition under Title II-C meet the needs of the larger research community, the Librarian of Congress has requested that the Title be amended to provide for the purchase of a second copy of everything acquired and to permit Library of Congress offices abroad to act as purchasing agents for other libraries. The second copy would be deposited in the Center for Research Libraries (see Recommendation 6), where it would be nationally available by loan or copy. For many foreign items such availability would be adequate, but every research library would continue to purchase material for its own collections; and the services of the Library of Congress offices, particularly in countries with no visible book trade, would be invaluable. Moreover, such a central service would eliminate the present necessity for expensive duplication of overseas procurement activities by many libraries. The Library of Congress would pay the administrative costs of acquisition, which frequently exceed the cost of the materials.

We strongly advocate the continuance and expansion of the Public Law 480 Program which is financed with counterpart funds and directly benefits a large number of American libraries. Between 1961 and 1967 this program distributed several thousand foreign publications to each of thirty-six American research libraries. The Library of Congress is capable of widening the program to include developing countries in Africa, Asia, and Latin America wherever counterpart funds are available and the Congress authorizes their use for research materials. We suggest that participating libraries be no longer required to make the payment that was imposed at the outset of the program.

The role of the Commission would be to weigh results, point to gaps in our foreign acquisition, propose administrative and legislative measures to expand and strengthen procurement programs, and exert every effort to stimulate the Federal support that the Library of Congress and other agencies will require if they are to fulfill their respective missions. The goal is that of the Farmington Plan: that at least one copy of every significant foreign publication be acquired and made available for use anywhere in the United States. The premise underlying this goal is even more evident now than it was in 1942 when a group of librarians stated it at a meeting in Farmington, Connecticut: There is no longer any part of the globe about which the United States can afford to remain in the dark.

BIBLIOGRAPHY

3. We recommend that the National Commission be given the authority to initiate and coordinate bibliographic programs through the establishment of a National Bibliographical Office and other means.[3]

The ideal of bibliography is to provide the scholar, wherever and whoever he is, with up-to-date information on the existence and location of materials relevant to his research, wherever they are. The turbulent outpouring of publication

[3] See Edwin E. Williams, "Bibliographical Control and Physical Dissemination," pp. 26–58, *infra*.

in recent years has made the ideal impossible to realize, and scholars in the humanities and social sciences in particular have been increasingly handicapped by what one of them has called "appalling arrearages" in cataloging and bibliographic analysis.

The Library of Congress now regularly performs an astonishing range of bibliographic services from the prompt cataloging of new American books to the *Monthly Index of Russian Accessions* and the current *National Union Catalog.* Funds for faster cataloging of more foreign titles have been authorized in recent legislation. In addition, scores of other libraries, agencies, and organizations are also producing bibliographies, indexes, and abstracts often of great value. Nevertheless, the breadth and depth of bibliographic analysis remains inadequate, with gaps in many fields; there is frequent duplication; and substantial delays, sometimes of years, continue to restrict the availability and adequacy of information about what has been published.

What is lacking and what is urgently needed is a National Bibliographical Office that can survey the nation's requirements, develop standards for bibliographical activities, eliminate duplication and waste; and support as necessary the filling of gaps. (See pp. 29–31.) Such an office would cooperate with the scholarly societies to promote abstracting and full indexing and to seek agreement on the data elements required to identify the several categories of research data to be included in machine processing.

But efforts such as those just outlined are directed primarily toward the cataloging and other forms of bibliographic control of new publications. We cannot ignore the equally important millions of publications containing the accumulated data, wisdom, and experience of the past already in our libraries. The Library of Congress has maintained for many years a National Union Catalog (NUC) of publications located in several hundred American libraries; but it is still an incomplete record of what is held even in this group, and it should be made more complete, both in depth and in extent. Publication of the catalog of all imprints before 1956 has begun, but ten years will be required to bring out the estimated six hundred volumes. Concomitantly, means should be found to complete this record of the essential older publications and make it available through the same automated techniques that will be used for the newer publications. Not to do so will result in imbalance in research, lead to wasteful duplication of expense as well as effort, and deprive the scholar of the improved service the computer offers.

We recommend also that the current Library of Congress bibliographic program relating to manuscripts and copies of manuscripts be further developed. Microphotographic reproduction of manuscripts and other unique materials serves both to make copies available to scholars throughout the country and the world and to prolong the life of the originals by saving them from unnecessary wear. Uncoordinated copying, however, results in wasteful duplication, and until now this has been the general practice. During 1965 the Library of Congress established the Center for the Coordination of Foreign Manuscript Copying to bring order into one sector of this vast field. We recommend that the Center's mandate be broadened to include the coordination of large-scale domestic photocopying as well. Information on what has already been done is being collected by the National Register of Microform Masters.

It is essential also that more nearly complete information be assembled on what exists in American manuscript collections. The *National Union Catalog of Manuscript Collections* (NUCMC) is in process of publication, and five volumes will be completed by the end of 1967; but at the present rate of progress the catalog will not be complete for years or even decades. Furthermore, hundreds of institutions with important manuscript holdings do not have the means to arrange, describe, and report what they have. In our view, Federal funds are required both to expedite publication of the NUCMC and to reimburse other libraries and historical societies for reporting their holdings.

There is a growing belief that many of the needs we have been detailing can be met by employing computer technology so that the bibliographical record can be "mechanically consolidated, manipulated, and rearranged to meet specific . . . needs." (See p. 30) Much research must be done before this expectation can be realized and the necessary support for it should be a primary concern of the National Bibliographical Office we propose.

TECHNOLOGY

4. *We recommend that the Commission plan, coordinate, and support research designed to improve library services through applications of modern technology.*[4]

In assuming responsibilty for library technology, the National Commission would be concerned with automation of library operations and bibliography, electronic communication among libraries, developments in microform technology, and such technical problems as the durability of book papers, film, and tape.

Promising technological experiments are being made in a few libraries across the country as noted elsewhere in this report (pp. 36–37). For a year the Library of Congress has been providing sixteen libraries with machine-readable cataloging data on magnetic tape (Project MARC) which has multiple utility, including the printing of catalog cards. The next step will be direct electronic linkage between a computer at the Library of Congress and computers in other libraries and information centers. But while there is progress toward a great national network, we know that such a goal is not likely to be reached overnight. To meet our society's virtually insatiable and infinitely varied demand for information, an effective national system must depend on a number of specialized networks; yet such networks are still in an ex-

[4] See Max V. Mathews and W. Stanley Brown, "Research Libraries and the New Technology," pp. 59–76, *infra.*

perimental state. Facsimile transmission is costly and as yet not very satisfactory. It is obvious that much more experimentation, research, and analysis of results will be required, not only to adapt present technology to library usage but finally to design systems that are workable and economically feasible. Greater effort and more funding will be required to move from pilot project to operating system, and national coordination will be vitally necessary to assure systems compatibility among libraries. At each step forward the National Commission would have a crucial part to play.

Microform production is another technology that has advanced rapidly in recent years, although it has not fulfilled Fremont Rider's prediction of 1944 that microtext would supplant the book. Nevertheless, every research library relies increasingly on various types of microforms. Microreproduction is particularly valuable for such bulky materials as newspaper files, for out-of-print works and for such specialized categories as technical reports. Here and there it is taking the place of books whose paper has deteriorated beyond usability. But more experiment and research are required to make these microforms more convenient, more legible, and more compatible with other media. (See pp. 66–69.)

For some years research libraries have been concerned with the problem of deteriorating books and other library materials. In 1964 the Association of Research Libraries outlined a plan for the preservation and continued availability of books of research value whose pages have become brittle. In 1967 the Library of Congress established an office to begin to carry out this plan. Further research and experimentation on methods of preservation may be a prerequisite to actual operations. (See pp. 42–43.) A useful function of the office would be to report periodically on the quality of paper going into current publications. The task of preservation will grow beyond bounds by the end of the century unless publishers adopt "permanent/durable" book papers. (See Recommendation 8.)

To carry out its mandate in this area the Commission may

decide that an Office of Library Research and Development is needed. However, the diversity and difficulty of the problems subsumed under technology may argue against their concentration in a single office and may argue for their respective assignment to existing agencies or institutions which have already progressed some way toward solutions. The main thought is that the single office, or the National Library Commission itself, would have a major role in guiding the library community along technologically promising paths to the future and in formulating solutions to problems that are essentially national in scope and clearly beyond the capacities of individual libraries. With such guidance and assistance the research libraries should be able to respond effectively to the rising demands that are being made upon them.

LIBRARY OF CONGRESS: THE NATIONAL LIBRARY

5. *We recommend that the Library of Congress be made The National Library by action of Congress, that it be named The Library of Congress: The National Library of the United States, and that an Advisory Board be created for it.*

Once no more than a collection of books for the exclusive use of Senators and Congressman, the Library of Congress has progressively devoted more and more of its program and operations to national needs and purposes. Since World War II it has become increasingly clear that the Library of Congress is performing many if not all the functions of a national library and that it is in fact the national library of the United States. We therefore recommend that the Library of Congress be now declared the national library by right and law. Furthermore, in order to give the new designation substantive as well as honorific significance we recommend that the Library of Congress be given the authority and means to become the keystone of a national library system and to take the lead in developing a worldwide library network.

To assist the Library in formulating policies and plans responsive to the research needs of the nation, we recommend the establishment of an advisory board to be appointed by the President with the advice and consent of the Senate. It is apparent from the discussion of the preceding recommendations that the Library of Congress, constituted as The National Library of the United States, will be the most appropriate agency to execute many of the research library programs to be delineated and promoted by the National Commission on Libraries and Archives. Specifically there are three important areas in which the contributions of the Library of Congress, impressive as they are, could be definitely increased were it given the responsibility and the means. They are the acquisition of foreign research materials on a global scale, bibliographical activities, and the application of modern technology. We are satisfied that what the Library of Congress could do in these and other areas as The National Library would immeasurably benefit not only Congress and the Executive Branch but the entire clientele of the country's research libraries.

THE CENTER FOR RESEARCH LIBRARIES

6. *We recommend that the Commission incorporate into The National Library System the facilities of the Center for Research Libraries and other cooperative programs that serve the national research interest, and that Federal support be provided to such agencies.*

Many of the needs for broader and faster access to research library materials can be satisfied most effectively and economically by a pool of such materials that can be borrowed (or photocopied) by any library as needed. In recognition of this, a group of university research libraries established the Center for Research Libraries in Chicago to collect and make readily available research materials for the joint use of scholars and scientists across the nation. The Library of Congress cannot provide the same ready access to its collections for scholars, wherever they may be, and at the same time fulfill its primary function of keeping the materials at hand and immediately available for the use of Congress and Federal agencies generally. The Center has been in operation since 1950 as a nonprofit institution, with the acquisition of research materials for nationwide loan and photocopy service as its primary purpose. The Commission's objective of improving access to more materials by more libraries can be most effectively and efficiently achieved by building on the Center's already substantial collections and experience. We therefore recommend that it be given Federal support to augment its income from members' dues and thereby enabled to provide ready access to materials that could not otherwise, or only at unnecessarily greater national expense, be made readily available to all research workers.

As noted earlier, legislation has been introduced with the support of the Library of Congress to amend Title II-C of the Higher Education Act of 1965 to permit the purchase of a second copy of significant current publications abroad to be deposited in the Center as a national loan copy. Federal support should be extended under the guidance of the Commission to include the purchase of retrospective materials and to cover related operations in the national interest. Under this arrangement the Center for Research Libraries would become in effect a national library for the dissemination of research materials. (See pp. 50–51.)

Similarly other nonprofit institutions able and willing to contribute significantly to the national library system should be appropriately supported. As already suggested, the Library of Congress may soon be fulfilling the original purpose of the Farmington Plan. However, Title II-C applies to current publications only, and there is therefore a sizable gap in foreign acquisition which the Farmington Plan committees are prepared to fill. Sponsored by the Association of Research

Libraries, these area committees have been purchasing retrospective research materials abroad and filming official documents and newspaper files that cannot be removed. They have actively collaborated with such scholarly organizations as the African Studies Asociation, and they utilize the Center for Research Libraries to house and make their growing collections available. This we consider a service vitally necessary to the research on which our understanding of the world depends, and we believe it clearly warrants governmental and foundation support.

The Association of Research Libraries has recently initiated a program of resource development on politically sensitive areas which is, in our view, deserving of substantial support. Founded in 1932, the Association has had a notable record, not only in diagnosing and prescribing for the ills of research libraries, but in devising projects and programs to enhance the value of library services to the research community. The Association has recently been given $500,000 by the Ford Foundation to perform bibliographical services and develop scholarly resources on Mainland China over a five-year period. This will begin to fill a lack in the field of Asian studies where bibliographical control has been inadequate and the competition for research materials has been marked by anarchy and duplication. In the planning stage, committees of the Association worked closely with committees of scholars, and control of the China project will be vested in a joint board of librarians and area specialists. The Association is prepared to extend its program to include the Soviet Union and Eastern Europe if funds are made available. In every case the Library of Congress will be depended on for acquisition wherever it has offices and adequate appropriations; but the Association centers will assume the duties of defining needs, abstracting, translation, indexing, and publishing bibliographical aids both for advanced scholarship and for undergraduate instruction.

What division of bibliographical labor would be agreed to between the Association of Research Libraries and the Library of Congress is conjectural; but the Library of Congress has accepted the principle of decentralization and sharing of responsibilties in proposing the Center for Research Libraries as a national lending library. It would seem wise to exploit fully the Association's initiative and special resources in certain sensitive areas.

COPYRIGHT AND THE NEW TECHNOLOGY

7. *We recommend that in revising the copyright law Congress postpone decisions relating to technological uses of copyrighted material until a national commission on copyright has made its report.*

The need for revising the present copyright law is widely recognized. In drafting new legislation Congress faces the difficult task of safeguarding the rights and interests of authors and publishers without creating obstacles to research or impeding the library services without which scholars would be unable to function. Modern technology has indeed introduced dilemmas in copyright theory and practice as is clearly set forth in Professor Ralph Brown's paper. (See Appendix.)

The doctrine of *fair use* of copyrighted material has grown up in response to the needs of scholars; we welcome the prospect that it will soon be explicitly authorized by statute, but we consider it essential that the scope and application of *fair use* should not be narrowed. We are alarmed to find that such narrowing is implied by the Report on House Resolution 2512[5] in spite of the intention of the Committee on the Judiciary, as stated in this report, to avoid "either freezing or changing the doctrine" (p. 31).

It would also be disastrous if the effect of new copyright legislation were to inhibit or hamper needlessly the development of improved services to research and teaching that the new technology is making possible.

[5] H. R. Report No. 83, 90th Congress, 1st Session, pp. 29–37.

There is virtually no body of data on current usage, and no one can foresee what will happen in this arena of constant change. Hence it is hard to see how legislation can be written today that will be satisfactory for years to come.

For this reason we advocate the establishment of a National Commission on New Technological Uses of Copyrighted Works as proposed in Senate Bill 2216, and we urge that no final decisions be made in this area until the Commission has made its report, three years after the date of the act. That report is to recommend legislation and administrative action designed to resolve the basic dilemma the new technology has brought into being. The eventual result of its findings might well be the establishment of a permanent commission to study the issues as circumstances change and recommend such changes in both law and administration as may from time to time be desirable.

PERMANENT/DURABLE PAPER

8. We recommend that the Government Printing Office and commercial publishers adopt lasting book papers for all publications of potential value in research.

When the Virginia State Library sounded an alarm about the "rapid embrittlement of modern book papers" in 1957, many American libraries were already beginning to microfilm and discard books whose pages broke when bent or powdered off when touched. This happened with books published since about 1870. Researches by the late William J. Barrow, financed by the Council on Library Resources, confirmed the opinion, first stated in 1829, that acidity is the primary cause of the deterioration of book papers whether they are rag or wood pulp. Mr. Barrow then went on to work out specifications for "permanent/durable" paper.

Mr. Barrow's findings led to a remarkable conference of librarians, publishers, paper manufacturers, and others in Washington in September 1960, and to subsequent developments which for a time promised that future librarians and scholars would be spared the scourge of brittle books. Two or three paper manufacturers announced their ability to supply nonacid papers, and two or three publishers adopted such papers. But the alarm gradually died down, and tests Mr. Barrow made just before his death in August 1967 revealed that most American publishers were still printing their books on paper that will lose its strength and flexibility before the end of the century.

If this practice continues, almost every current library accession will impose a needless burden on the staff and budgets of the next generation of librarians. One American research library is now spending eight or nine dollars to microfilm an average-length book that can no longer be handled, its total filming costs threaten its budget for book buying, and the growing backlog of books waiting to be filmed are of no use to anyone and divert the staff from other duties.

To bring about the general adoption of permanent/durable paper for publications of research value, scholars and librarians must make publishers fully and constantly aware of the disastrous consequences their use of acid book papers has entrained. We believe also that the changeover might be facilitated if the Library Commission we propose were to get publishers and paper manufacturers to agree on the specifications for permanent/durable papers and then get librarians and scholars to specify the categories of publications they consider worthy of longevity.

In appealing to publishers to adopt enduring book papers we recall that President Johnson asked the National Advisory Commission on Libraries to recommend actions by both public and private groups that would increase the adequacy and effectiveness of the nation's libraries. In our view the publishers of America would make a contribution of incalculable magnitude to the functioning of research libraries by simply printing their books on paper that will last centuries rather than decades.

SUPPORT: THE PRIVATE SECTOR

9. We recommend that corporations and foundations provide increased support for research libraries.

We are convinced that the nation's research libraries must receive a larger share of the national income if they are to meet the insistent demands that are made upon them. The Executive Order establishing the National Advisory Commission on Libraries specifically calls for recommendations for action by private institutions and organizations as well as by the government. In our view, research libraries would be on solid ground in seeking financial assistance from foundations and corporations.

The Foundation Directory[6] reports that 6,803 foundations made grants totaling $1,212,000,000 in 1966 and that grants have been increasing at the rate of 16 percent a year. While research libraries received a very insubstantial part of this total, scores of well-endowed foundations, on the basis of their stated purpose and objectives, should be receptive to appeals in support of carefully designed library projects and programs, including experimentation which would not necessarily be financed otherwise.

More pointedly, a number of foundations have liberally subsidized scholarship through grants-in-aid and fellowships but with an occasional notable exception their benefactions have overlooked the research libraries upon which their grantees have depended. Foundations have also made substantial grants to universities to establish and operate research centers and to strengthen the curriculum in neglected areas. All such grants should include substantial support for the libraries upon whose resources and services both instruction and research depend.

Another welcome type of foundation support would be grants for projects and programs of benefit to all research

[6] The Foundation Library Center, *The Foundation Directory,* Edition 3. New York: Russell Sage Foundation, 1967.

libraries. An outstanding example is the Council on Library Resources which was established by the Ford Foundation in 1956 to solve the "problems of libraries generally, and research libraries in particular." During the presidency of Verner W. Clapp, the Council supported an astonishing range of projects including basic research on several of the librarian's most baffling problems.[7]

Corporate giving to higher education has increased several hundred percent in the past ten years, as necessity has improved the techniques of university fund-raisers and the Council for Financial Aid to Education has alerted the corporate world to frequently alarming college and university deficits. The fact is, however, that corporations could increase their contributions some four hundred percent before they reach their tax-deductible limits. In most cases the university librarian will not make his own appeal for corporate support but will provide his president with a statement of needs and projects for inclusion in a university appeal. We particularly commend corporate support as a source of income to the unaffiliated research libraries. It need hardly be said that corporations that rely on research turn constantly to the general research libraries, and this suggests that the libraries' appeal to them need not be phrased wholly in terms of altruism.

SUPPORT: STATE AND LOCAL GOVERNMENTS[8]

10. We recommend that the several states and local governments adequately support their university libraries in the interest of education and research, promote state and regional

[7] Council on Library Resources, *Tenth Annual Report*, Washington, 1967.

[8] We are indebted to Kenneth E. Beasley for facts and insights incorporated in this section. Mr. Beasley wrote a paper for the ACLS Committee on "Library Service and State Governments" while director of the Research Department of the Kansas Legislative Council. He is now head of the Political Science Department at the University of Texas at El Paso.

networks, and assist libraries whose collections have special significance to their states or regions.

In spite of growing Federal aid to research libraries, enlightened self-interest should persuade the states to maintain or increase their support of research library services. This they could do on a modest scale by automatically providing for library support in all state programs pertaining to education, health, transportation, urban blight, etc. In our view, also, when they establish library systems, the states should recompense research libraries for the additional services they will have to assume. But the main item will undoubtedly continue to be support of the state university library or libraries.

It is a truism to say that graduate instruction that is worthy of the name requires a well-stocked, growing library, and we know that the budget of such a library may increase more rapidly than that of any other part of the university. The states will have more to spend each year—state expenditures in the aggregate are expected to rise from 75 billion dollars in 1965 to almost twice that amount in 1975—but the competition for every dollar will be determined and intense. To compete successfully, the state university librarian will have to convince his president that his fiscal requests are warranted and cannot be postponed; the president will then have to convince the governor, and the governor the legislature, while at each step there will be competing interests, each with its own peculiar merits. But the librarian has an excellent case in the rapid expansion of enrollment since World War II, the particular impact of greatly increased graduate study, the proliferation of new areas of research and instruction with their demand for instant collections, and sharply rising library costs. The case is not self-evident, however, and it must be repeated and constantly documented by a continuing flow of information on the library's needs, plans, and prospects.

The new university or new branch of an existing university faces a particularly difficult task for it will require the simultaneous acquisition of retrospective and current materials of all types: books, periodicals, newspapers. How costly this may be is suggested in the expenditures for library materials of new branches of the University of California at San Diego and of the State University of New York at Stony Brook. Neither institution has as yet more than the beginning of a graduate school, but in 1966–1967 each spent more than a million dollars for books. Each has set one million volumes as its initial goal.

The university president and the legislators may well inquire whether such dramatic costs can be cut down or offset by more borrowing of books or by the creation of automated networks. Although there are successful cooperative arrangements by which the faculties and libraries of several colleges have in effect been pooled, the state university must depend very largely upon its own resources. As the university librarian at San Diego recently reported, experience has proved "conclusively and repeatedly" that borrowing cannot be relied upon except for the very unusual and little used items.

Several states have begun the planning and experiment which will lead to library networks of varying mesh; but experience so far has indicated that the benefits will have to be measured in services rather than in savings, even after massive initial capital investments. Furthermore, we feel that there is a real danger that a preoccupation with networks or systems may divert attention from the need for sustained resource development. A library must have resources and services beyond the requirements of its own immediate users if it is to share; and the strongest libraries could be seriously disrupted and weakened if they were required to satisfy the unclassified wants of numerous smaller libraries. New York State has foreseen this danger and has established fees which the state pays both for inquiries and for loans or copies. In the design of state or regional systems we strongly advise that adequate compensation be provided for the additional reference and lending load a few research libraries will inevitably carry. A Federal contribution such as that provided in the Library Services and Construction Act of 1964 will be essential and Federal participation at the planning stage will ensure the requisite compatibility with other and larger library systems.

We commend the enterprise of the states that are now fashioning library systems for themselves or for their regions. Without awaiting the outcome of their efforts, we can be sure that a network that is functioning well would be capable of providing bibliographical services far superior to any we now have, and that in the next stage it would increase the availability of the identified material in its original form, in microcopy, or on a screen.

The Federal government has largely overlooked the unaffiliated libraries that cannot be classified under higher education. They may have priceless treasures and provide the materials for magnificent scholarship; but they have no alumni and no visible means of support beyond an endowment which may have to be cut into to wipe out current deficits. Certain historical societies and independent libraries can validate a claim to support by the states and the localities whose heritage they richly document.

SUPPORT: THE FEDERAL GOVERNMENT

11. We recommend that the Federal government extend existing legislation and provide adequate funds to enable research libraries to respond more effectively to the nation's requirements in all areas of scholarship and inquiry.

Since World War II, and particularly since the advent of the space age, the nation's research libraries have been all but overwhelmed by the proliferation of publication on every continent and by mounting demands on their resources and services from the universities, the industrial community, and research centers supported by government contracts. Librarians have been keenly aware of this dual pressure, and they have taken what corrective measures they could. But there has been no assurance that their isolated efforts would be more than palliatives or that they would finally coalesce into a functioning national system. Furthermore, what had to be done was simply beyond their resources. In their statement to the National Advisory Commission on Libraries in January 1967, spokesmen for the Association of Research Libraries expressed their belief that more Federal support "must be brought to bear" because the libraries themselves, singly or in concert, lack the financial capability to deal with "the research library problem."

Research libraries have had very modest Federal support in the past, but their importance to the nation's welfare was specifically attested in the Higher Education Act of 1965. Title II of that Act was designed to strengthen the resources of research libraries and to ease their predicament. In our opinion certain amendments to the Act would enhance its usefulness to the libraries and the several communities they serve.

Title II-A provides for grants for the purchase of books and other library materials for academic but not for independent libraries. We believe that all research libraries should benefit from Title II-A as they do from Title II-C. While the unaffiliated libraries have no enrolled students, their collections are in constant use, most of them serve the faculties of widely scattered colleges and universities, and some of them, notably the New York Public Library, might be mistaken in term-time or vacation for any crowded university library.

The Association of Research Libraries has recommended that the supplemental grants in Title II-A be based not on total university enrollment but on a count which weights graduate students by a factor of four, in view of the heavy demands they make on the library's resources and services. We consider this a sensible suggestion. We believe also that following its survey of library needs the National Commission will recommend that the sums authorized and appropriated under Title II-A be substantially increased.

The Federal government has provided indispensable support to the training of librarians in Title II-B, and in consequence there has been a heartening increase in enrollment in library schools. However, an increase in the number of trained librarians would not necessarily meet the distinctive requirements of research libraries. Meager financial and administrative support has generally forced the library school to operate within a narrow band and to emphasize training rather than scholarship. Greater support would enable the schools to broaden their aims and courses of study, and devise ways and means to produce the rare hybrid that every research library seeks, the librarian-scholar, either by divided graduate programs or by courses in librarianship specifically designed for linguistic or area specialists.

We have already indicated our approval of amendments broadening the scope of Title II-C. In this and in other instances the unsolved problem is how to persuade appropriation committees to view library needs with the same understanding and sense of urgency that education committees evince. Authorization is often less than half the battle. In the case of Title II-C the Library of Congress was authorized to acquire research materials on a global scale and catalog them without delay. Although the Library of Congress prepared itself for its expanded role in both acquisition and cataloging, appropriations have fallen substantially below the authorization, and the full intent of the act has not been realized. In this area the National Commission will have a useful part to play.

We believe that the Congress should provide funds for related library support in all legislation that authorizes or creates fellowships, grants-in-aid, and contracts which directly or indirectly depend on library services.

We trust that Federal funds will continue to be available in support of regional systems, with the stipulations that compatibility and eventual linkage with a national library system are provided for, and that libraries that carry more than their share of increased services are compensated for them.

We believe also that Federal as well as foundation funds should be used to establish mutually beneficial relations between research libraries here and abroad, to promote the overseas programs of such agencies as the United States Book Exchange, for the exchange of library personnel, and for the expansion of the Shared Cataloging Program of the Library of Congress in the interest of standardization and compatibility in the exchange of bibliographical information on a worldwide basis. When funds are appropriated to carry out the purposes of the International Education Act, specific library support should be added.

Finally, if the Administration and the Congress establish and suppport the central structure we have proposed, namely a continuing National Commission and a Library of Congress functioning as the National Library in the full sense of the name, the nation's research libraries will be enabled to forge a coherent library system which will effectively meet our needs as a nation and a people.

Edwin E. Williams

Associate University Librarian, Harvard University
Cambridge, Massachusetts

II

Bibliographical Control and Physical Dissemination

Research can be defined as studious investigation directed toward the extension of knowledge. Obviously it must build on what is already known. It may require expeditions to unexplored regions of the earth or beyond, laboratory experimentation, or study of the collections in galleries and museums; the sources of knowledge are as varied as knowledge itself. Almost always, however, research depends in part (and often it depends almost wholly) on libraries. Almost always, likewise, the results of research are reported in written, printed, or other records that libraries collect, organize, and make available to scholars.

Research libraries have helped to create modern civilization; their strength and vigor directly affect the health of scholarship and hence of society as a whole. The rapidly growing abundance of knowledge, which would have been impossible without research libraries, now confronts them with far more difficult tasks than ever before.

This abundance is reflected by striking quantitative increases in publishing; the output in many fields is now doubling every seven to ten years. There are new forms of publication, many of them difficult to obtain and to organize, and they are now produced by every inhabited area of the earth. Traditional boundaries between subject fields are breaking down, so fewer scholars now find that highly specialized collections are adequate to meet most of their needs. Moreover, traditional methods of collecting and organizing research materials are too slow to satisfy these needs.

The demands upon research libraries are made by a rapidly growing clientele. In 1870, less than a century ago, there were 5,553 faculty members in American institutions of higher education; by 1962 there were 424,862. One Ph.D. was earned in 1870; there were 382 in 1900, 2,299 in 1930, 3,290 in 1940, 6,633 in 1950, 9,829 in 1960, 11,622 in 1962, and 14,490 in 1964. Scholars engaged in formal postdoctoral work are now more numerous than graduate students working for the doctorate were until a few years ago. A study made during 1960 indicated that there were then some 10,000 postdoctoral scholars (most of them in the sciences and in medicine, and most of them supported by Federal funds) in addition to perhaps 15,000 medical interns and residents, college teachers, and visiting faculty. It can be anticipated that the National Research Council's Study of Postdoctoral Education, which is now under way, will reveal a substantial increase in numbers during the past seven years, and the rate of increase should accelerate for years to come. This is yet another result of the speed at which knowledge is growing; postdoctoral study is becoming essential for professional scholars and those in more and more callings that demand constant upgrading and updating of knowledge. Those who teach in colleges and universities are by no means the only scholars whose research is producing the new knowledge that will shape the future; research materials are as essential to the industrial as to the academic community, and research libraries are essential to economic as well as to cultural development.

Fortunately the increased demands of scholars come at a time when the opportunities are also unprecedented—most notably those opportunities that arise from automation and other technological advances, and those that stem from increasing recognition of scholarship and of research libraries as national resources that must be nationally supported. Needs must be assessed and plans must be made.

BIBLIOGRAPHY IN GENERAL

Collecting by libraries is essential, but it is equally essential that there be bibliographical apparatus by means of which the scholar can learn of the existence and location of materials that may be useful to him. The catalogs and classification systems of libraries, important as they are, meet only a fraction of scholarship's needs; research depends also upon periodical indexes and abstracting services, national and subject bibliographies, and a multitude of other records of what has been written.

The latest edition of Besterman's *World Bibliography of Bibliographies,* though it excludes general library catalogs and all bibliographies that are not separate publications, lists 117,187 volumes of bibliography under 15,829 headings. Four years ago the Library of Congress prepared a *Guide to the World's Abstracting and Indexing Services in Science and Technology* listing 1,855 works that were then currently appearing at regular intervals. It is not easy to enumerate even all the major kinds of bibliography. Some bibliographies, like the 1,855 just mentioned, are current serials that attempt to provide information as promptly as possible on recent publications; others are restricted to works prior to a given date. Some attempt to include everything in their field; others are selective and critical. Some list titles only; others include annotations or extensive abstracts. Some list works only under the names of their authors; others list them under subject headings or in classified arrangements. Some confine themselves to books; others are restricted to articles in periodicals. Despite the international character of scholarship, national bibliographies are among the most ambitious and most useful achievements in recording what has been published; it is unfortunate that such bibliographies are still lacking for many countries.

Many bibliographies give no indication of where the scholar may obtain copies of the works they list; but library catalogs are among the major species of bibliography, and some of the outstanding subject bibliographies are catalogs of single great collections. Union catalogs and lists also include some of the greatest achievements of bibliography. The National Union Catalog at the Library of Congress has demonstrated that a great unpublished bibliography existing in a single copy can be highly useful, but its contribution to research will be greatly increased when its publication in book form, which is now under way, has been completed and it can be consulted in libraries throughout the world. Finally, it should be observed that not all published bibliographies appear as books or periodicals; alternative forms include cards, microfilms, and now magnetic tapes and other machine-readable media.

No one nation is going to do all the world's bibliographical work; no one agency or type of agency is going to do all the bibliographical work of the United States. Government departments, libraries, professional societies, and commercial publishers will continue to produce bibliographies, and this diversity ought to serve the constantly changing needs of scholarship better than any monolithic system. Yet coordination is an obvious need; the field of bibliography has become so vast that it is difficult to obtain the information on which decisions and plans ought to be based. At present the Federal government has no bibliographical policy, and no one is responsible even for a continuing survey of the growing bibliographical output of the government, much of which fails to meet recognized bibliographical standards. There is no comprehensive and systematic effort to collect, appraise, and disseminate information on current developments in the application of computers to bibliographical work, yet these developments seem to offer the best grounds that scholarship has for hopes that bibliography can after all succeed in keeping track of the rising output of recorded knowledge. As library catalogs, bibliographies, indexes, and abstracting services are automated, it is vital that their machine-readable stores of information be compatible. Lack of uniformity in present book-form bibliographies may do relatively little harm, but a great advantage of converting bibliographical information to machine-readable form is that it can be mechanically consolidated, manipulated, and rearranged to meet specific local needs. Only a vigorous and extremely well-informed effort can hope to assist and persuade the host of organizations that produce bibliographies to cooperate for the benefit of scholarship as a whole.

Consequently a National Bibliographical Office ought to be created. This, as has been emphasized, is not envisaged as a regulatory agency in any sense, but as a central source of information on which voluntary coordination can be based, an advisory body identifying needs and formulating bibliographical standards, a referral center for bibliographical inquiries, and possibly, under contract, an agency for making special searches and compiling bibliographies.

This Office would have international as well as domestic responsibilities; it should work closely with UNESCO and other international agencies as well as with bibliographical centers in other countries. Here it should be kept in mind that assistance to foreign bibliographical undertakings directly aids American research and American libraries; when any other nation establishes a good national bibliography, for example, it benefits scholarship everywhere

Domestically the Office should supplement rather than supplant effective existing agencies such as the Office of Science Information Service of the National Science Foundation, which "is responsible for providing leadership among non-Federal science information services, and in developing appropriate relationships between Federal and non-Federal activities," its objective being "to supplement internal Federal information activities, and insure that scientists and other users have ready availability to the world's current and past output of significant scientific and technical literature."[9] In medicine, with the National Library of Medicine, and in other scientific fields a great bibliographical advance is now under way. MEDLARS, the National Library of Medicine's Medical Literature Analysis and Retrieval System, stores citations to a portion of the world's biomedical literature on magnetic tapes and retrieves information electronically, making individual "demand" searches, producing bibliographies, and printing the *Index Medicus* by means of a computer-driven phototypesetter. Decentralization has now begun with the establishment of regional search centers to which tapes are supplied. The National Science Foundation reported in 1965 that national science information systems now appear to be within reach, and the same report announced that the American Chemical Society had contracted for a two-year program for mechanized information services; under this $2,043,600 contract, 800,000 chemical references are to be fed into the system. The Foundation suggested that this arrangement might well be a prototype for future Government–scientific society relationships. It has been observed that bibliographies are produced and supported by a wide variety of agencies, but it ought to be emphasized that the scholars in each field cannot expect to be well served bibliographically unless they determine and make known their needs; hence their own organizations, the professional and learned societies, have a clear responsibility for leadership here.

The Office of Education has now inaugurated ERIC (Educational Research Information Center) with a center in Washington and twelve clearinghouses in universities and other institutions throughout the country, each with responsibility for covering a specific subdivision of research in problems of education, such as junior colleges, counseling and guidance, exceptional children, or educational administration. These clearinghouses acquire, select, abstract, and

[9] National Science Foundation, *Annual Report*, 1965, p. xviii.

index relevant documents; the center stores full texts of documents on microfilm, announces all new acquisitions, and makes copies available at nominal cost. Important data-archive projects such as the Inter-university Consortium for Political Research at Michigan and the Roper Public Opinion Research Center at Williams College, should also be noted, but the sciences, where pressure is greatest and where financial support has been relatively easier to obtain than in other fields, can be expected to lead the way in comprehensive and automated bibliography. Other areas of scholarship must be assisted to follow.

LIBRARY CATALOGING

Subject bibliography and information systems involve analysis in depth of the content of publications, and it is evident that urgently needed improvements in present services will require continued efforts by learned societies and other organizations as well as by libraries. Library catalogs, since they deal for the most part with whole volumes, may seem less complex, but the listing and classification of millions of books in a great library—or in the libraries of the nation—is not a simple matter. Cataloging at present is often too slow to serve the needs of scholarship, and libraries can ill afford to waste their inadequate supply of trained manpower on the duplication of work that far too often is still required. A great step forward in library cataloging ought to result from the Higher Education Act of 1965, which authorized a proposal by the Association of Research Libraries for expanding the foreign acquisition and shared cataloging programs of the Library of Congress. Under this legislation (which authorized sums of $5,000,000 for 1965/66, $6,315,000 for 1966/67, and $7,770,000 for 1967/68, but for which fully adequate appropriations were not or have not yet been voted) the Library of Congress is to acquire, as far as possible, all library materials of value to scholarship that are currently published throughout the world and promptly to provide catalog information for these materials. This is by no means an easy task, but the efforts made thus far are already enabling American research libraries substantially to reduce their duplication of work and hence to save money as well as to give better service to scholars by speeding up their cataloging.

At a later point in this memorandum something will be said of developments that may grow out of the acquisitions part of this program; here it should be noted that the new program promises to contribute to bibliographical progress internationally and to library automation. The Library of Congress has been collaborating with foreign national libraries and national bibliographies in setting up its machinery for acquisition and cataloging. American libraries are beginning to use cataloging done abroad, and the result is to reduce duplication of effort internationally as well as within the United States.

In addition to the efforts in acquisition and cataloging that it is making under the Higher Education Act of 1965, the Library of Congress, in cooperation with a few research libraries, is experimenting in the dissemination and use of cataloging data in machine-readable form. Research library records, for acquisition and circulation functions as well as for cataloging, have long been based on cards; now, as the transformation to a computer-based record system gets under way, it is essential that compatible methods be adopted. In other words, computers in each research library must soon be prepared to incorporate into its system information received from computers at the Library of Congress and elsewhere, just as, in the past, it was possible to incorporate printed cards of standard format into card catalogs. It is to be hoped also that the new computer age will lead to more standardization internationally than has been achieved in library cataloging up to now.

Whatever else research libraries do in the immediate future, they can afford to let nothing take precedence over the effort to move ahead with the shared cataloging program that has been launched under the Higher Education Act of 1965. This is not to suggest, however, that all major problems of research library cataloging can be solved by this program or that other efforts are not required. It deals with current publications and hence must emphasize the speedy transmission of data, which makes it all the more desirable to automate procedures as soon as possible; but research library catalogs contain millions of cards listing publications of past years, and research libraries must continue to acquire and catalog such publications by the thousands. The largest libraries do this as they strengthen their great collections by filling in the gaps, while a multitude of new or relatively weak libraries must attempt to build up research collections adequate to meet the growing needs of their scholarly communities.

A major advance in this vast field of retrospective cataloging was assured recently when the American Library Association was able to announce the completion of arrangements for publication in more than 600 volumes of the National Union Catalog's record of books published prior to 1956. (The record for publications since that date has already been published, and is kept up to date by monthly supplements with annual and quinquennial cumulations.) This colossal publishing project, the largest ever undertaken anywhere, has been planned and contracted for without governmental or foundation subvention. It will disseminate a store of bibliographical data accumulated since 1901, when the Library of Congress began to print catalog cards and to exchange them for those printed by other libraries. A Rockefeller grant enabled the Catalog to add more than 6,300,000 cards between 1927 and 1932; major American research libraries have been reporting their acquisitions for many years, and there are now some 16,-500,000 cards recording locations of books in 800 libraries of the United States and Canada. Hitherto this information has been available only in the single card file at the Library of Congress; its publication will enable scholars to locate books without directing inquiries there, and will give catalogers in each subscribing library access to catalog information for more than ten million publications. In selection and acquisition it will be of great value in identification of books and, more important still, it will enable libraries to avoid needless duplication of books already held by other American collections. Costs of editing and publication will be paid by subscribing libraries.

The National Union Catalog's record of American research library holdings is far from complete and far from impeccable. It has not been automated. Something better would be possible a few years from now, but postponement of publication would have meant that, for some years to come, scholarship and research libraries would have had to do without the incomplete and imperfect but highly useful catalog that can now be made available. It should be added that provision has been made for changing the "printer's copy" during the course of publication from cards to machine-produced output at any time when this becomes practicable, so the undertaking will not entail any delay in automation. Eventually the American National Union Catalog should be consolidated with similar records of research library holdings in other countries.

Clearly it is now reasonable to expect that research library catalogs will eventually move from card files into computerized form, but it is unrealistic to suppose that this will come as a single step; the beginning, presumably, will be made with data for current publications. This might well be followed by putting the Library of Congress catalog onto computer tapes (or their successors) and enabling other research libraries to draw from the tapes, for their own automated catalogs, data for those books of which they have copies. At the same time, they would add to the tapes data for those of their holdings that were not represented at the Library of Congress. This procedure would minimize duplication of effort in putting catalog data into machine-readable form; eventually it would also produce a completed, revised, and greatly improved National Union Catalog. This Catalog, since it presumably could be consulted electronically from a distance or through duplicate local stores of machine-readable data, might never need to be reproduced and disseminated in book form.

Completion of the National Union Catalog would deserve a very high priority even if it could not be done with the help of computers, and even if it could not be regarded in part as a by-product of research on library automation; its value to the scholar who works with noncurrent publications can hardly be overestimated. The effort to complete it should not be confined to the incorporation of a record of holdings of large research libraries; many other collections, particularly those of historical societies, possess books of great value for the study of America's past that are to be found nowhere else.

An attempt to set up a timetable for this mechanization of research library catalogs would seem premature until present experiments in the transmission of data for current publications have led to an effective program for supplying machine-readable data in conjunction with the shared cataloging project. Valuable experience is also being accumulated as work continues on projects such as Harvard's shelflist automation, the University of Chicago's "integrated, computer-based, bibliographical data system," and Project INTREX at the Massachusetts Institute of Technology. Harvard is transferring its handwritten, loose-leaf shelflist to machine-readable punched cards and publishing printouts that the computer produces in three sequences: a classified arrangement, alphabetically by author, and chronologically by date of publication. Chicago, with the help of a National Science Foundation grant, is attempting to combine into a computer-accessible, permanent record all elements of information about each book or other bibliographical item added to the library; the stored information will be used for many purposes: to determine holdings, prepare orders, maintain acquisition files, generate acquisition lists, prepare charge cards and labels, and produce full sets of catalog cards. M.I.T. is experimenting with its 125,000-volume Engineering Library in providing scholars with remote access to a computer-controlled magnetic memory store of bibliographical information on books and other library materials; consultation is to be through consoles linked to a central computer by ordinary telephone lines.

Costs of installing automated systems may seem high, but costs of operating these systems compare favorably with those of operating the present manual systems, and the scholar can be expected to benefit greatly from the improvements and innovations in service that automation can produce. The 1963 study of *Automation and the Library of Congress* estimated the costs of conversion to an automated system at $50,000,000 to $70,000,000, but operating costs of the system in 1972 were forecast at $4,500,000, compared with $5,000,000 for the present system and its substantially less satisfactory services. Other libraries, incorporating into their systems machine-readable bibliographical data produced by the Library of Congress, should have relatively lower costs of conversion and operation, and the scholars who use them should benefit enormously from access to an automated national system as well as from the increased accessibility of local holdings.

Despite its magnitude, the National Union Catalog is by no means the only important source of information on the location of research library materials, and it must continue to be supplemented by publications such as the *Union List of Serials*, which contains more than 225,000 entries describing periodical and other serial holdings of 680 libraries in the United States and Canada. Its current supplement is *New Serial Titles*, and the Library of Congress, having completed publication of the Union List's third edition, is now planning a World Inventory of Serials in Machine Readable Form, as recommended by the Association of Research Libraries. When completed, such an inventory would be a tool of inestimable scope and utility. The next step would be a union list of serials in machine-readable form, the additional information being, of course, locations.

Further improvements in the system for reporting and disseminating the record of serial holdings are needed. Other important aids to the scholar in finding specialized types of material include *Newspapers on Microfilm,* the *Union List of Microfilms,* the *Guide to Archives and Manuscripts in the United States* (now seriously out of date), the *National Union Catalog of Manuscript Collections,* and services like the new Center for the Coordination of Foreign Manuscript Copying. The Library of Congress is also maintaining a National Register of Microcopy Masters and is disseminating lists based on this, but there is as yet only rudimentary machinery for the coordination of copying or for supporting the massive program of copying both books and manuscripts that would be highly desirable.

Guides to the location of materials in American libraries such as those that have been mentioned have numerous foreign counterparts, and the development of microfilming facilities abroad is making it increasingly easy for American scholars to obtain copies of library holdings wherever they may be. The demand for copying rises sharply as information regarding manuscripts becomes more readily available.

It should not be forgotten that manuscripts are by no means the only important type of material omitted from both the National Union Catalog and the *Union List of Serials.* Union lists of African, Russian, and Latin American newspapers have appeared during the past fifteen years, but there is no source of information on holdings of most foreign newspapers, and Winifred Gregory's *American Newspapers, 1821–1936,* now thirty years old, has not been brought up to date. Neither has her *List of the Serial Publications of Foreign Governments, 1815–1931.* Publications of great importance in special fields—sheet music and art exhibition catalogs, for example—have largely escaped the bibliographical net, to say nothing of maps and nonwritten materials such as sound recordings and photographs of all kinds.

COLLECTING AND COLLECTIONS

It may seem illogical to have considered bibliography and library cataloging before dealing with library collections, on which many bibliographies and all catalogs must be based. The scholar, however, normally approaches research materials through bibliographies and catalogs. Moreover, the work of selection and acquisition that builds any research collection must depend in large measure on bibliographies and on catalogs of other research collections. This was the case even when libraries were more self-sufficient than they are today; as it is, the sharing of information and of physical materials is so fundamental to research library operation that one cannot intelligently discuss collections and collection-building without constantly keeping in mind the bibliographical apparatus that makes each individual research library part of a much larger, though as yet imperfectly articulated, library organism that extends beyond local and even national boundaries.

The members that make up this organism have been called research libraries, but it needs to be kept in mind that this term covers a multitude of diverse institutions, many of which are not exclusively engaged in supporting research. The small college library serves research needs of its faculty to the extent that it can; the large university library is heavily used by undergraduate students as well as by professors. Some state and municipal public libraries have important research materials; there are still proprietary libraries like the Boston Athenaeum with outstanding collections, and a number of major libraries, including the American Antiquarian Society, Folger Shakespeare, Huntington, Library Company of Philadelphia, Linda Hall, Morgan, and Newberry, that depend largely if not wholly on endowments and gifts for their support but continue to make their resources available to an increasing number of scholars under increasing difficulties.

The Reference Department of the New York Public Library is among the largest and most significant institutions in the country. Its holdings (that is, those of the Reference Department alone, which is not supported by taxation, in contrast to the Circulation Department of New York Public Library) are surpassed in extent only by those of the Library of Congress, Harvard, and Yale, and they are unequaled in many subjects, yet funds available for services, current acquisitions, and preservation of the collections are becoming more and more inadequate; endowment is being used up in order to keep the Library going.

The current *American Library Directory* lists more than 7,700 specialized libraries in the United States, some 2,000 of which form part of university or other library systems. The total includes 1,231 medical, 571 law, and 246 religious libraries, and collections on scores of other subjects, maintained by government agencies, private industry, and associations of all kinds. There are special libraries with more than one million volumes—the National Library of Medicine, National Agricultural Library, and Harvard Law School Library—but it should be emphasized that a relatively small, highly specialized collection may also contain important research materials. Notable examples, as has already been suggested, are many historical society libraries possessing manuscripts and other unique documents of inestimable value for the study of history.

Research libraries, then, are of many kinds, and research materials are more varied still. Much has been written during the past few years of how difficult it is to collect and organize the rapidly growing abundance of scientific publications. The difficulties are indeed great, and they will not easily be overcome; but the difficulties of collecting and controlling research materials for history and other social and humanistic subjects are far greater. At the risk of oversimplification, chemists may be contrasted with historians. The record of research done by other chemists and by scientists in related fields is what the chemist normally needs to consult. There are far more research chemists than there used to be, yet they form a relatively limited and identifiable group. Their writings are issued by publishers who intend to disseminate them to scientists and to the libraries used by scientists. These writings now appear in "near print" and in technical reports as well as in the books and journals published by academic institutions, laboratories, learned societies, governments, industrial corporations, and commercial publishers. As has been said, collection and control of this literature is no longer easy; yet the chemist's needs are of a strikingly different order from those of the historian.

Like the chemist, the historian needs access to all the relevant writings of his scholarly colleagues. But his method of adding to this body of knowledge is not laboratory experimentation like the chemist's; it is to search and sift materials of all kinds that were not produced by historians or, for the most part, issued for the use of historians. The latest and most up-to-date compilation of information in his field cannot provide all that he needs, for historical literature is noncumulative and older writings never become completely obsolete. He may find useful data in a newspaper or pamphlet, an advertising leaflet or a schoolbook, a dime novel or a sermon, a photograph, tape recording, correspondence file, or personal account book. The memoranda or working papers prepared for use within a government department may be much more illuminating than its published reports. Perhaps it should be noted also that, if the report of a chemical experiment is lost, it is possible to duplicate the experiment; but when the last copy of a printed book or the unique copy of a manuscript diary is destroyed, some portion of the record is erased forever.

Selection and acquisition of materials to serve research of this kind can never have been a simple matter, and the difficulties have multiplied as the interests of American scholarship have extended to all areas of the earth. When American research in the humanities and social sciences was largely focused on the United States and Western Europe (and when these areas also produced nearly all the world's scientific and scholarly literature), American libraries could identify much of what they needed in good bibliographies and obtain much of it from an established publishing industry and from dealers who specialized in supplying libraries. In many of the countries that are now of particular interest to American scholars, it is almost impossible to discover what has been printed or to obtain copies unless a library can send its representative to scan the shelves of bookshops and deal personally with officials of the government departments that issue useful publications.

The world's publishing output has not been listed nor, indeed, has it been counted; there are no reliable statistics even for books and journals. The Library of Congress was adding more than 300,000 volumes and pamphlets per year *before* expanded foreign acquisitions began under the Higher Education Act of 1965, and the largest university libraries, though some of them acquire 200,000 books per year at a cost of more than $1,000,000, find their collections less and less adequate to meet the current demands of teaching and research. Hence American research libraries have sought Federal assistance. In 1962 appropriations authorized by an amendment (Section 104-n of 1958) to Public Law 480 (of 1954) enabled the Library of Congress to begin to use foreign currencies from the sale of surplus agricultural commodities for buying and distributing to American libraries current books, periodicals, and related materials. Though few countries have as yet been included in this program, it has clearly demonstrated the desirability of establishing acquisitions agencies in countries lacking a well-organized publishing industry and book trade. Now, as the Library of Congress augments its foreign acquisitions program under the Higher Education Act of 1965, it evidently should be enabled to make its acquisitions facilities available to other libraries. (Appropriate legislation is now before the Congress.)

Regardless of the assistance that it may be possible for them to obtain from the Library of Congress, research libraries will need to continue cooperative efforts in foreign purchasing. Publications that are unobtainable commercially can often be acquired by exchange, which also provides useful American books and periodicals for many foreign institutions that cannot get dollars for buying in the United States. It has often been recommended that each country establish a national exchange center, and the UNESCO *Bulletin for Libraries* lists thirty-nine such national centers. Though the Smithsonian Institution has long functioned as a shipping agency for international exchanges, the United States has no national center, and funds ought to be provided to enable the United States Book Exchange (USBE), a nonprofit clearinghouse sponsored by major American library associations, to serve as the American national center. As such, it would maintain up-to-date information on current American and foreign serial publications that are available for exchange from the libraries of universities and other institutions, assist in arranging direct exchanges between institutions, and extend its duplicate clearinghouse activities to foreign libraries, which cannot for the most part afford the service charges that are necessary so long as USBE must be self-supporting. It is unfortunate that in 1963 the Agency for International Development terminated the program under which USBE had supplied more than 2,500,000 books and journals to 1,800 foreign libraries during the preceding nine years at a cost to AID of some $1,500,000 for service charges. A revived and expanded program of this kind ought to be supported; in addition, the program for information and service as an exchange intermediary that has been recommended could be financed for some $150,000 per year.

It should be emphasized that the acquisition of new

publications is not enough to build the research collections required by American scholarship. The largest and oldest libraries constantly discover gaps in their collections, even the best of their collections, that ought to be filled in, and, as new programs develop in their institutions, they are frequently called upon to support research in fields that hitherto had been neglected. There are more new and rapidly developing universities than ever before, and all of these, if they are not to be seriously handicapped by inadequate libraries, must build up extensive retrospective collections in many subjects. There are great differences here between the needs of one scholar and the next; many a scientist and many a specialist in such contemporary problems as economic development may rarely need to consult a publication that is more than five or ten years old. For such men, a library with a good program of current acquisitions may soon become adequate. In the case of many other scholars, regardless of all that can be obtained by borrowing or photocopying, no equally useful substitute is now in sight for the great retrospective collections that traditionally have required decades and even generations for libraries to assemble.

The oldest and largest American university library is at Harvard, where a recent planning study estimated that the University's library collection (7,600,357 volumes in 1966) would grow to more than 10,000,000 volumes in 1976, and that annual expenditures for the library ($6,728,455 for 1965/66) would increase to $14,655,000 in 1975/76. These estimates were based upon surveys of student and faculty needs, and took account of substantial savings anticipated from automation and increasingly effective library cooperation; the actual rate of increase in expenditures for the past eleven years has been greater than was predicted for the next eleven. It has also recently been estimated that within ten to fifteen years there will be sixty to seventy universities in the United States with graduate programs of real quality. Each, presumably, will need to acquire current publications on a scale comparable to Harvard's, and some of them at least, in an effort to increase the relative strength of their retrospective collections, can be expected to spend more than Harvard on the acquisition and organization of non-current publications.

It has been emphasized that research libraries are diverse and numerous, but it would be a mistake to overlook the particular significance of the libraries of major universities, both those now in existence and those that can be expected to reach maturity during the coming decade. It is these libraries in which most of the nation's scholars—most of those who teach the teachers and most of those who add to the store of human knowledge—receive their advanced training.

Even when funds are provided very generously, the new institutions find that it takes enormous effort and considerable time to build great collections. Some desirable books rarely come on the market, and the competition for all useful out-of-print books is increasing, which has its natural effect on their prices. This competition, incidentally, is both domestic and foreign, since new universities are by no means an exclusively American phenomenon. Theoretically it would be possible to argue that the new institutions have been born too late, should specialize in research that normally requires only recent publications, and ought to leave old books to their elders. However, if this theory had been adopted a century ago, all the great research libraries would be in Europe; if it had been adopted a generation later, it would have restricted American research libraries to the Eastern seaboard.

The reasonable assumption, therefore, is that traditional library collecting ought to continue and will continue. The problem is how best to supplement it, how to reduce as much as possible the disadvantage under which scholars in new institutions would labor for years to come if they had to depend entirely upon the slow traditional processes of collection building. Something will be said in the next section of this memorandum regarding plans for coordination and sharing of resources. First, however, substitutes for original books ought to be considered.

These substitutes are provided by photographic reproduction in all its forms. The market provided by hundreds of new colleges and universities has stimulated a vigorous republication industry, which is bringing back into print many important books. Obviously the works that are reprinted are those of which the most copies can be sold, so needs of the college library and of undergraduate instruction are more likely than the specialized needs of advanced research to be met in this way.

For small editions, particularly for small editions of voluminous sets or collections, microphotographic reproduction is evidently more likely to be practicable than full-size republication. Recognizing the fact that scholarship can no longer afford to depend almost wholly on commercial sources for reprints or for microform projects, the Association of Research Libraries has recently established a program to improve access to materials that currently can be obtained from mainland China only in unique copies or very small quantities. Supported by a grant of $500,000 from the Ford Foundation, this program will identify texts that are of interest to the scholarly community and make them available in a variety of formats, ranging from microforms available on loan to offset reprints. The Association is now investigating the possibility of extending its Scholarly Resources Development Program to other areas of the world such as Africa and the Slavic nations.

With modern reader-printer machines that will immediately produce a full-size copy of pages selected by the scholar, the disadvantages of having to work with microreproductions can be considerably reduced. The lack of an integrated system of library copying has delayed and seriously limited the exploitation by scholarship of the potentialities of microreproduction. Essential features of such an integrated system are outlined in the chapter of this report dealing with Library Automation; they include quick and automatic conversion apparatus for all forms of copying, microforms readily manipulable by hand and by machine, automatic conversion to microform of machine-readable information, and microforms that facilitate immediate access to each page of text as well as rapid scanning of many pages. It should not be forgotten, however, that some scholars, notably those engaged in bibliographical investigations of how texts were printed and of their vicissitudes in successive editions, must examine originals, and that many others may be seriously impeded by the inconvenience of having to depend on microfilm reading machines and the impossibility of browsing through the shelves of a collection arranged according to a systematic subject classification. On the other hand, it should be observed also that the largest and strongest libraries are relying to an increasing degree on microreproduction, both to supplement their collections and to replace publications that have physically disintegrated.

No problem confronting major research libraries is more alarming than the deterioration of paper, and nothing short of a comprehensive national effort will suffice to deal with it. The oldest books, on the whole, are surviving much better than most recent publications; the paper that was used for more than four hundred years after the invention of printing was remarkably durable. About a century ago, however, there was a great change with the adoption of certain acid-sizing processes in the manufacture of paper and with increasing use of wood pulp; as the result, a very large proportion of the books printed during the past hundred years are rapidly becoming too brittle to use and many are already crumbling into dust. In 1965 the Association of Research Libraries adopted in principle a plan based on investigations financed by the Council on Library Resources. This calls for a national center that would preserve, in so far as possible, the best example of each deteriorating book deposited with it, would maintain a collection of master microfilm negatives, and would disseminate photographic copies (both microphotographic and full-size) to libraries. The total cost of the program during its first ten years was estimated at slightly less than $10,000,000.

A preliminary study of procedures for identification of materials is now under way at the Library of Congress. Establishment of the National Register of Microcopy Masters there was also an important development because it provides information that is essential if libraries are to minimize needless duplication of filming for preservation as well as for other purposes, but nothing has yet been done to ensure the preservation of master negatives, which ought to be in the custody of a national center or of research libraries. These negatives must conform to high standards and must not be exposed to the hazards of use except for making positive microcopies; likewise it is essential that they be permanently available for this whenever a scholar may need such a copy.

An effective national center for preservation and dissemination of research library materials would seem to be the appropriate agency to coordinate copying projects of all kinds. The need for coordination and for support of such projects has been mentioned apropos of the National Register of Microcopy Masters and other bibliographical services, and it has been noted that the Association of Research Libraries has now launched a Scholarly Resources Development Program in order to supplement commercial copying. A national center, with the full cooperation of research libraries, could in effect bring back into print all books held by these libraries, and the benefit to scholarship throughout the nation—to scholars based in the old and large libraries as well as to those in new institutions—would be hard to overestimate.

Further steps should be taken as soon as possible to put the A.R.L. plan of 1965 into effect, and continued research is needed on several questions, including optimum storage conditions for the books that are to be preserved, practicable methods of deacidification that will retard the disintegration of books now on research library shelves, the durability of film copies, and the chemistry and thermodynamics of paper. Very preliminary reports of current research at the University of Chicago suggest that deacidification may soon be practicable on a large scale, which would be an enormous boon to individual libraries and would help to make the national program more effective.

Every effort should also be made to induce publishers to use permanent/durable paper for the books that libraries will be acquiring during the coming century, and organizations representing the scholarly community ought to launch a vigorous campaign.

COORDINATION AND SHARING OF RESOURCES

From bibliography to the proposed center for preservation and dissemination of research materials on distintegrating paper, this memorandum has dealt repeatedly with cooperative or centralized activities. In a sense, all the research collections of the world form a single great library; certainly the holdings of American research libraries constitute a national collection that is more a functioning entity than an abstraction. Scholars depend on many of the same bibliographies regardless of which unit of the national collection they may be using. Each unit has on its shelves the catalogs of many others, and can refer to union catalogs giving the locations of millions of volumes that are not in its own stacks; each uses, and hopes in the future to use far more effectively, cataloging done elsewhere. There are joint acquisition projects, copies of whole collections in other library units are acquired on film, and there must be a joint attack on the menace of disintegrating paper. In addition, each major library lends thousands of volumes annually to others and borrows thousands for its own community. Microfilms and other photocopies are being produced in rapidly growing numbers as a substitute for loans. Finally, each major library attracts hundreds of visiting scholars each year.

There are many flaws in the organization. It is expensive to obtain copies of books; photographic and interlibrary loan services are far too slow; and there are too many uncertainties. Even so, the scholar who knows that a book he needs is in a distant research library can usually obtain a copy, and the sources of information through which he can learn it is there are being improved. Most of the suggestions that have been made here for strengthening American research libraries would do so by improving the national system and taking advantage of the opportunities now offered by automation.

When resources are shared to the extent that they have been for many years, each research library benefits directly as their total increases. It does not gain much from those books in other libraries that duplicate its own holdings, but it can and does draw upon collections that supplement its own. This inevitably suggests the possibility of specialization in collecting, and some sixty American research libraries have now been participating for twenty years in the Farmington Plan, under which each has agreed to collect current foreign books intensively in certain fields. Each, in other words, has undertaken to acquire more, in the areas for which it has accepted responsibility, than would be selected if only the needs of its own institution were taken into account; in return, each has the assurance that a similarly inclusive collection in every other subject is being built up by one of the other participants, from whom it can borrow.

The time now seems to have come for considering changes in this plan in the light of another major cooperative achievement, the Center for Research Libraries in Chicago. This began as the Midwest Inter-Library Center, a regional organization for acquiring and housing infrequently used publications, but modern communications make collections of books and microfilms in Chicago almost as accessible to new members of the Center in Vancouver, Cambridge, and Los Angeles as to its original participants in Minneapolis and Columbus.

Now, as has been noted, it is hoped that the Library of Congress, under provisions of the Higher Education Act of 1965, will acquire current foreign publications comprehensively—more comprehensively, it is reasonable to expect, than individual Farmington Plan participants have been successful in doing. If the Library of Congress can acquire two copies of each new publication and forward one of these to the Center for Research Libraries, the Center might function as a national lending library, and individual responsibilities under the Farmington Plan could then be discontinued. Would a centralized national collection be preferable to the decentralized one that is now being created by Farmington Plan specialization? An affirmative answer seems to be justified by the fact that it would no longer be necessary to guess how a book had been classified for purposes of Farmington Plan allocation or to consult the National Union Catalog to determine the location of recent foreign publications, and that centralization of responsibility should make possible better service (in cataloging, in interlibrary lending, and in filming) than can be expected from sixty individual libraries, each of which has primary obligations to its own community. (Indeed, a few of the participating libraries cannot lend publications, and can only provide photocopies.) If centralization is desirable, should it be at the Center for Research Libraries rather than at the Library of Congress? Here it may be observed that the Center is an instrument of American research libraries and is responsible to them, while the Library of Congress naturally must continue to give priority to service to the Congress and to agencies of the Federal government. A certain measure of insurance would also be provided by having two collections rather than one. The United Kingdom, it may be noted, has supplemented the British Museum, its great noncirculating national research library, by establishing two separate institutions specifically for circulation and dissemination: the National Central Library and the National Lending Library for Science and Technology. The former has a relatively small collection (less than 400,000 volumes) of its own but maintains a large union catalog and is the center of the national interlibrary loan system. The latter, dealing primarily with periodicals, currently receives 30,000 serials; it undertakes to handle loan requests the day they are received and to send out photocopies the day after orders reach it.

The Farmington Plan has been the major national effort

in specialization by American research libraries; hence it might appear that disillusionment with specialization is implied by the proposal to include Farmington Plan collecting among the national services that the Center for Research Libraries should be assisted to develop. In fact, however, as has been indicated, this proposal for centralization is prompted by the desire to make the nation's comprehensive collection of current foreign publications as accessible as possible. It should be emphasized that, even when maximum accessibility has been achieved, the existence of this national collection will not relieve each research library of the need to build a strong collection of its own to serve its own community.

There is evidence that specialization and cooperative effort are becoming increasingly desirable at the local and regional levels. One reason for this is that there are more universities. Few metropolitan areas have had more than a single genuine university or a single major research library. Soon, however, there will be few such areas without a number of institutions conducting substantial research programs. This suggests the possibility of local agreements to specialize in collecting as well as the development of central research collections to supplement the other academic libraries in a metropolitan area. Here, as in other programs for sharing and increasing resources, the special problem of the college (as distinguished from university) professor should be kept in mind; the undergraduate college cannot build up research collections, yet many members of college faculties need access to such collections for their own scholarly research.

Locally as well as nationally there are limits, of course, to the extent to which any institution can depend on central collections and on those of libraries with which it may share responsibility under agreements for specialization in collecting. Each university library must support the changing research programs of its own university, and no university can or should undertake to forgo certain specified subjects for all time and to continue forever to emphasize certain others; indeed, the individual scholar sometimes finds that his investigations have led him to areas in which he had not expected to require strong library resources. Each institution must plan, but must also be prepared to modify decisions regarding what must be collected on its own shelves and what can properly be left to other collections either national or local.

It seems evident that scholars will depend more and more upon microtexts and other photographic copies. The many new institutions must acquire photocopies of millions of volumes that are no longer available in any other form, and older research libraries have millions of volumes on their shelves that will soon, if they have not already, become too brittle for normal use. An increasing number of scholars will live at a distance from major research collections. The largest libraries can acquire a constantly decreasing percentage of the total output of the world's presses, and consequently will rely to a growing degree upon other collections such as the national lending library that has been proposed. If much of the increased use of microcopies is inevitable, there are also many cases in which choices can be made between lending and filming, between storing immense collections of books and substituting microcopies plus, of course, the reading machines required for their use. Investigation of both research needs and of economic factors must provide information on the basis of which intelligent choices can be made. Thus the Center for Research Libraries, under a grant from the National Science Foundation, is now studying the costs and service characteristics of alternative methods of making journal literature available to scientists. There must be further studies of this kind, and there must be periodic re-examinations of the problem in the light of technological developments, particularly in the area of high-reduction techniques, which promise to make it possible to reproduce multiple copies of large collections at relatively very low cost. Difficult copyright questions are involved. So are questions relating to fees for use and their effect on scholarship; libraries traditionally have absorbed the costs of interlibrary loan, but with a few exceptions, notably the National Library of Medicine, have charged for photographic copies supplied in lieu of loan.

Something has been said of the limitations of microphotographic reproductions as substitutes for original books, and it should be added that, while everything practicable ought to be done to aid scholars in institutions that do not have great library collections, there is little prospect that any substitutes can serve the scholar quite as well as a great collection on his subject located where he is working. It is one thing to search bibliographies and catalogs and to request that books be supplied on loan or in film or other copies; it is another to live with a great collection, freely able to look into scores of books shelved next to the ones that have been identified through bibliographies and catalogs. We must not fail to support such collections. As barriers to access are reduced and a national network is perfected, it must be emphasized that the strength of the network depends on the strength of the outstanding collections that it links.

GENERAL OBSERVATIONS

As the problems of access to recorded knowledge are considered and as efforts are made to facilitate the scholar's access, it may be well to keep in mind certain general principles.

First, balance ought to be maintained, and progress is needed along more than a single line. New institutions must be assisted to build collections of their own and to draw readily upon the resources of older and larger libraries. Important as this is, it would be a mistake to concentrate all efforts upon helping the new and the weak; we must build upon strength and maintain the quality of existing great collections while creating the new ones that are now urgently needed. All libraries benefit from further strengthening of the outstanding research collections on which all depend to supplement their own holdings, just as all benefit from improvement of bibliographical apparatus, research in the application of automation to library operations, and cooperative projects in cataloging and acquisition. It should be kept in mind that most research libraries are now hard pressed to maintain the collections and services required by their own particular constituencies; they cannot be expected to provide greatly increased regional or national services unless means can be found to reimburse them for the additional costs of these services. The nation's first great universities and great libraries were built by private benefactions; a few state governments have had the vision and the resources to emulate this example. Now, as the time has come when Federal funds must supplement private donations and state appropriations in supporting research and research libraries, the gravest mistake that could be made—yet, unfortunately, perhaps the most natural—would be to neglect the institutions that are strongest and seem relatively affluent.

Second, existing services and procedures must not be abandoned until better services and procedures are in operation. Scholars must be supplied with research materials today and tomorrow; service cannot be suspended while systems are installed that will provide much better service the year after next. Present libraries are sometimes described as obsolete; perhaps this is really praise, for there is a saying in technological circles, "If it works, it's obsolete." One can almost always assert that, with the technology that may then be available, a project might be done better next year than it can be done now; but to wait for this reason means never to do anything. Publication of the National Union Catalog is an example; rather than wait, it seemed preferable to do the imperfect job that can be done with present machinery, particularly since embarking on the project now did not preclude a change to better machinery during the course of publication.

Finally, without losing sight of the diversity of scholarship and of the materials it requires, all research libraries should be alert to opportunities for profiting from the advances that are being made by specialized scientific libraries. The National Library of Medicine is collecting comprehensively, producing the great bibliography in its field, sharing its resources with medical libraries throughout the nation, and pioneering in the development of automated procedures. The Medical Library Assistance Act of 1965 has made provision for a comprehensive program, including assistance in library building, instruction, special projects, research and development, improvement of basic library resources, publication, development of a national system, establishment of regional search centers, and possibly a branch of the National Library of Medicine. The authorization was for $23,000,000 per year, and the budget of the National Library of Medicine is now approximately $6,000,000 per year. These are not extravagant sums, it would seem, in view of the contributions that this program should make to teaching and research in the medical sciences.

National library service and national programs for development should be practicable in other subjects. It has been noted that the National Science Foundation has contracted with the American Chemical Society for mechanized information services, and this suggests that services like those of the National Library of Medicine might in some cases be provided by contract between a Federal agency and an existing non-Federal library.

The President's Science Advisory Committee found in 1963 that "Since strong science and technology is a national necessity, and adequate communication is a prerequisite for strong science and technology, the health of the technical communication system must be a concern of Government." It was good that science and technology led the way in 1963; establishment of the National Foundation on the Arts and the Humanities, modest as its resources are thus far, seems to demonstrate that the nation now realizes that scholarship and research as a whole are national necessities. It must likewise be recognized that research libraries are the indispensable basis for an adequate communication system in all fields of scholarship. The increasing concern of Government is inevitable and it is welcome, but this must be accompanied by increasing concern also on the part of private organizations and individuals. The natural sciences and, to a lesser extent, the social sciences have been fortunate in having an industrial constituency to demand that bibliographical and library resources be provided, and to help in financing these resources. The humanities must enlist private support on a comparable scale; equal opportunity for research in all fields of knowledge is essential for the healthy growth of scholarship and for the civilization that scholarship builds.

RECAPITULATION

How can American scholars be supplied with the information they will need during the coming decade?

Much that is now being done must continue with increased support and at an accelerated rate:

Support of numerous useful current bibliographies, indexes, and abstracting services.

Maintenance of the strength of existing strong libraries, and rapid development of the additional strong collections that will be needed for a total of sixty to seventy universities with graduate programs of real quality.

Strong emphasis on Library of Congress programs for shared cataloging, increased foreign acquisitions, and sharing of acquisition facilities with research libraries.

A variety of experiments in library automation.

Publication of the present National Union Catalog and improvement of supplementary guides to the location of research materials; there must be no delay in making information on serial holdings readily available through a machine-readable *Union List of Serials.*

Several innovations are essential:

Creation of a National Bibliographical Office to promote coordination of effort in this vast area.

Provision for a number of subjects of bibliographical services and information systems like these now being developed for a few scientific fields.

Study of needs and bibliographical planning in all fields, with leadership from the professional and learned societies.

Completion of the National Union Catalog by the incorporation in it of a record of all significant American research collections.

Dissemination to research libraries in machine-readable form of the bibliographical information contained in the National Union Catalog.

Automation of bibliographical systems and research library operations as rapidly as proves feasible.

Extension of responsibilities of the Center for the Coordination of Manuscript Copying to include American as well as foreign materials.

Development of a National Exchange Center at the United States Book Exchange.

A program for preservation and dissemination of materials on deteriorating paper along the lines proposed by the Association of Research Libraries.

Use of durable paper by publishers.

Creation of a National Lending Library, supplemented by regional centers.

Continuing study and experimentation is required throughout; two areas need particular attention:

Periodic re-examination of the bibliographical needs of each research field in the light of changes in the field and new developments in technology.

The economics of microphotography and the use of microcopies, taking into account both the changing needs of scholarship and the changing state of the art.

Max V. Mathews
Director, Behavioral Research Laboratory
W. Stanley Brown
Head, Mathematical and Information Systems Research Department
Bell Telephone Laboratories
Murray Hill, New Jersey

III

Research Libraries and the New Technology

INTRODUCTION

The nation's research libraries are threatened by the rising stream of publication and they are not likely to save themselves without the help of technology, and in particular varying degrees of automation. But automation of any existing process is a complex change with many pitfalls that must be approached with great care. The germane question is not how to automate libraries but rather what processes of libraries, if any, will be improved by automation. The huge storehouses of material in libraries are hard to change and would themselves resist the sweeping restructuring which any attempt to achieve complete automation would entail. Research libraries are large and varied collections which we wish to preserve, and this puts an additional requirement on plans for automation. Except for a few special cases concerning new fields that have no body of retrospective literature, we must plot a viable, evolutionary path along which present collections can be made more useful for research by means of automation technology. Desirable as certain ends may be, they will remain hypothetical Utopias unless we can foresee a course of development. Hence, a legitimate and essential question, which must always be asked as part of any plan, is "How do we proceed from our present libraries?"

We must avoid errors of both overconservatism and over-optimism in applying new technology. Libraries are so important and expensive that we must overlook no possible savings in cost or increase in effectiveness which can be furthered by technology. On the other hand, we cannot afford the very expensive mistake of relying on technology which does not exist and may never be created. Neither can libraries themselves be expected to develop extensive new technology.

From this point of view, it seems reasonable to discuss the next steps in library development which can be taken over the next ten years, and which use foreseeable modifications of existing technology. The considerations will be organized into three aspects: computer technology and machine-readable information, microform technology and copying, and means for interactions between libraries. All aspects are interrelated and each will develop its full potential only if the others follow the course outlined.

Our concentration on relatively secure goals should in no sense be interpreted as a rejection of "venture" research of an advanced nature. Computer "understanding" of natural languages, automatic abstracting, optical readers capable of reading any book from the shelf, economical long-distance facsimile transmission of entire books, and other similar developments deserve attention when and if research and experiment solve their basic problems. Current and realistic library plans must not require the success of these projects.

COMPUTER TECHNOLOGY

The impact of computer technology on libraries will be felt in two different directions: (1) improving bibliographic access or assisting the library user to obtain information, and (2) automating library operations. In the first area, machine-readable catalogs will assist research by making widely available multiple copies of the catalog, subcatalogs, and union catalogs. In the second area, the prime candidates for automation are acquisition, circulation, and inventory control.

A card catalog is a remarkable invention. It can be used to locate one document among millions. It is simultaneously accessible to many users. It can be edited and kept reasonably accurate. However, one cannot use it without going to the one place where it exists. This explains the current interest in catalogs in book form, on microfilm, and on magnetic tape, all of which can be made available wherever they are needed.

A magnetic tape catalog is well within the capabilities of current technology, and it has striking advantages over the other types of catalog. The original card catalog can be kept up-to-date. The catalogs in book form or on microfilm cannot be kept up-to-date, though supplements can be added; and they do not lend themselves to any but the simplest search. Magnetic tape has many advantages. It can be constantly updated, it can be restructured in several different ways to facilitate different search strategies, it can be used to make humanly readable microform catalogs, and two or more tapes can be automatically merged to produce a union catalog.

The magnetic tape catalog does not allow either librarians or library users to search the complete catalog in real time because of the time necessary to mount and spin tapes. Real-time access may become possible with a large enough on-line storage device which may be available within a few years. The feasibility of using it depends on the cost and on the availability of an appropriate computing system. Fortunately, real-time access is not essential to any of our major purposes, since all needs for rapid access to the complete catalog can be fulfilled by the printed or microform version. Making the conservative assumption that the machine-readable catalog exists solely on magnetic tape, we shall now discuss its uses, its construction, and the associated costs.

To the library user, a catalog is for "searching." We distinguish between two fundamentally different types of searches. An easy search is one that requires the examination of only a very small portion of the catalog; for example, a search in the author catalog for a book whose author is known. A hard search is one that requires the examination of most or all of the catalog; for example, a search for all books whose titles contain a particular word. Easy searches must be rapid, and need not involve a computer. Hard searches must involve a computer, but need not be rapid. Because of their cost, hard searches will be batched. It would be unreasonable to do them daily, but they could be carried out weekly or monthly depending on the demand and the urgency.

Sometimes a hard search can be made easy by resorting and restructuring the catalog. For example, a search by title in an author catalog would be hard, but this catalog can be resorted and restructured into a title catalog, thereby making all subsequent title searches easy. Similarly, a search for titles containing a given word is hard in a conventional catalog but easy in a permuted index. (Unfortunately, the sheer bulk of a "permuted catalog" might be a serious obstacle to its construction and use.)

We turn now to the construction of the machine-readable catalog. Clearly we cannot ask that the old catalog be converted suddenly into machine-readable form. What we can do is to begin to automate the processes of acquisition and circulation, and to grow a machine-readable catalog as a byproduct. If each item that is acquired, copied, or loaned is entered into the machine-readable catalog, then it will not be long before all items that are new or frequently used will be included.

This type of catalog will not meet the needs of all scholars. One of the characteristics of research, particularly in the humanities and social sciences, is its requirement for access to many library materials that are neither new nor frequently used. Knowledge advances by building on the accumulated data and wisdom of the past, and improved access to this body of literature is no less needed than improved access to what is being currently published. Attention must therefore be given to finding an economically viable method of making the old catalog, that is, the existing catalog of existing literature, widely available in machine-readable form. Few individual libraries can afford the capital cost of completely converting their own catalogs, and the duplication of holdings between libraries would make such individual effort wasteful. Still, the unique holdings of every research library should be listed on tape for the national benefit. This is a national problem for which a number of solutions have been proposed. One of course is completing and converting the National Union Catalog, even while it is in process of publication in six hundred volumes.

Next, let us consider the cost of a machine-readable catalog and the costs of the associated operations which we have been discussing. In order to get some feeling for magnitudes, we shall consider the library at the University of Chicago which has almost two and one-half million volumes. The card catalog contains about five million cards of 300 characters each. Fuller description of each document would be as desirable in the machine-readable catalog as in the card version, and would greatly increase its value to the scholar. In the listing of costs, conversion is omitted because the assumption is that this occurs as a by-product of automated processing and circulation. However, the cost of getting a single catalog card into a computer has been estimated at 35 to 42 cents; and for the entire catalog this cost alone will have highly deterrent effect.

1. The machine-readable catalog would occupy about 80 reels of magnetic tape, worth about $5000 ($60 per reel).

2. One pass through the catalog would take about 5 hours of computer time (4 minutes per reel), and would cost about

$1000 ($12 per reel). During this pass, one could edit the catalog, make several updated copies, and perform several exhaustive searches to assemble valuable subcatalogs.

3. A complete resorting of the catalog would take about 32 hours of computer time (24 minutes per reel), and would cost about $5800 ($72 per reel). For a much smaller catalog (less than 10 reels), the time would be 20 minutes per reel and the cost would be $60 per reel. For a larger catalog (more than 100 reels), the time would be 28 minutes per reel and the cost would be $84 per reel.

4. A microfilm version of the catalog would occupy about 30,000 feet of 16mm film (or 10,000 4″ × 6″ microfiches), worth about $1500.

5. A microfilm version of the catalog could be generated from the machine-readable version in about 10 hours at a cost of about $1000, plus the cost of the film.

6. A microfilm version of the catalog could be copied photographically, and would therefore cost little more than the cost of the film.

7. A paper version of the catalog, with characters of the size found in a telephone directory, would occupy 100,000 pages. A crude estimate for generating a few copies is $3000 per copy based on 3-cents per page copying cost. This does not include binding costs.

These figures give an indication of both the possibilities and the limitations of a machine-readable catalog. It would be reasonable to revise it, make updated copies, and perform complete searches to assemble valuable subcatalogs, but this could only be done on a weekly or monthly basis. It would be possible to re-sort and restructure it for major purposes, but this could not be undertaken lightly. A microfilm version could be published once or twice yearly. Supplements would be necessary.

From these estimates it seems to us that machine-readable catalogs will be very useful, and will not flounder even in very large libraries. However, they will only make sense if they are used carefully in the proper ways.

Now let us consider automating library operations: acquisition, circulation, and inventory control. Manual methods for performing these operations are barely able to cope with libraries of existing size. Automation is essential if the size of libraries continues to expand. Furthermore, highly effective programs appear feasible with present computers.

The most important point in the automation of acquisition is that one machine-readable description of a document, possibly prepared by the publisher, may be the major input to an over-all program that ends with the document available to library users, several entries for it in the main catalog (or more likely in the current supplement), and the bill checked and paid.

Circulation and inventory control are different aspects of the general problem of keeping track of library holdings. In principle the borrowing and returning of documents could be recorded directly in the machine-readable catalog, if it were kept in on-line storage. Fortunately a separate small machine-readable catalog of currently borrowed items will serve equally well. This would, for example, permit the automatic generation of overdue notices.

How can a good set of computer programs be created for libraries? They must be built up gradually by experimental development in an existing library. With focused objectives and effort, progress should be clear in a period of perhaps five years. Some programming experts must be brought into libraries but, more important, librarians must learn to use computers and must come to understand their strengths and limitations. This education process will take several years under the best conditions. From experience in other fields we can emphasize that there is no alternative to *library experts learning computation*. Any other course will lead to inferior results with great waste of money and effort.

What kind of computation centers will be best for libraries?

For acquisition, a little time on a local computer in batch processing mode will suffice. For keeping track of circulation, a small amount of time-shared computing will be required. It may also be desirable to keep subcatalogs in on-line storage at a local computing center. In this case also, time-shared access will be essential. Fortunately, libraries will not need to have their own computers for any of these purposes.

For processes involving the entire machine-readable catalog, or a major portion of it, we believe it will prove advantageous to establish special library computation centers. The normal computation facility serving a university community is not well suited to the economic processing of large catalogs. A regional library computation center could serve perhaps ten or twelve libraries. The computing system at one of these centers will have a large number of tape drives (perhaps twenty), and a large but relatively slow memory. The tape catalogs will probably be kept at these centers, since they will be safer there and they would be of little or no use elsewhere.

MICROFORM AND COPYING TECHNOLOGY

We believe microform and copying technology will be at least as important in libraries as computer technology. For example, in the instances where cost and copyright are not overriding factors, full-size copying machines have already revolutionized circulation habits. Needless to say, copying technology will interact strongly with computer technology and will affect the entire structure of library automation.

The importance of this technology results from its impact on the storage, handling, cost, and circulation of library holdings. These factors will always be fundamental in libraries. Storage space will be reduced, handling by machine (as well as by people) will be made possible, cost of a document will be reduced, and circulation will be pushed in the direction of copying rather than borrowing.

As will be clear from subsequent details, microforms will supplement rather than replace conventional library holdings.

Some materials cannot usefully be photographed. All materials will be available as or convertible to conventional hard copy. Hence, the user who specified conventional books, either for objective reasons or for subjective preference, must continue to be satisfied. It is usually too costly for individual libraries to convert extensive hard copy holdings to microfilm form. However, there is a growing microfilm publication business. Many periodicals and a number of books can be purchased directly in microform; new libraries turn to microfilm for out-of-print books; crowded libraries save space by putting bulky materials on film.

In contrast to full-size copying machines, why is the adoption of microforms so much slower? There is undoubtedly reader resistance, though there is some evidence that the established scholar is more insistent on the original than the graduate student, and high school students are the microfilm's warmest friends. But we believe that the answer is simply that no overall system which is properly engineered for the reader has been assembled. However, almost all the pieces of such a system already exist and the overall system could be created with a little well-directed encouragement of existing companies plus a little standardization. Listing a few requirements will clarify our concept of such a system. We envision three forms of information, full-size hard copy, microforms, and machine-readable digital tapes.

1. Quick, automatic apparatus must be available for copying any of these forms and for converting from any one of them to any other.[10] There are three cases of copying and six cases of conversion, as illustrated in Table 1. A full-size, high-quality, dry sheet of paper should be produced from a microform in seconds. Further, a sequence of sheets should be generated automatically without manual intervention between pages. Immediate output is not as essential in converting from

[10] Reading by an optical scanner is possible only in special cases, and the free convertibility here described depends on the development of a satisfactory general-purpose optical scanner.

TABLE 1. *Modes of Copying and Conversion*

From \ To	paper	microfilm	machine-readable
paper	copy	photograph and reduce	read page
microform	enlarge	copy	read micropage
machine-readable	print	microprint	copy

full size to microform, but the process should have a high speed to minimize costs. Microform copies of anything must be immediately available to customers in the library or for interlibrary loans. They should be automatically produced. The quality of images must be such that several generations of copies can be made without serious degradation.

Methods for publishing machine-readable information are especially vital. Microform copies will be preferred in many cases. Present microfilm recorders for computers come very close to meeting library requirements.

2. Microforms must be hand and machine manipulable. None should be so small or delicate that it cannot be hand carried. They must have a shape such that a simple and cheap machine can store, move, and look through any aggregate. Labels which can be read with the unaided human eye and by a simple machine must be an inherent part.

3. Some must be mailable. Much interlibrary communication will be by microform. These must be suitable for mailing: light, flat, and not brittle.

4. The microforms should be humanly readable in simple apparatus. Further, it should be possible to scan pages with as much facility as scanning a book. More specifically we

envision an entire book imaged onto a few "cards" that can be mass-produced, handled and filed easily, reproduced easily, and read comfortably. Any page should be immediately accessible and it should be possible to scan rapidly through many pages. The cards should be labeled for both people and machines.

What is the state of development of microform apparatus to satisfy the requirements we have just posed? Some version of all machines exists, except possibly for a microform camera-processor to produce immediate microforms from hard copy, and this would not be hard to create. Excellent and rapid microfilm printers for computers exist (see the Appendix to this chapter, p. 75, for an example). Additional "human engineering" is needed on many components. Some "machine engineering" is needed to add machine-readable labels to all microforms.

The most pressing need is for standardization and completeness. By standardization we do not mean one huge machine that will do everything on one kind of microform. A multiplicity of smaller machines is preferable from all standpoints, and rolls, "cards," and aperture cards are probably a minimum number of different forms to handle different functions. However, machines should be obtainable to convert from one form to another.

How long and how much money will be needed to make these machines available? We have not been able to get an estimate from companies in the microform business. A way to promote the development of this system is to create a small laboratory of four or five workers. About half their effort would be spent for their own research, the other half would be spent prodding the microform industry by means of contracts pointed at specific objectives. The laboratory costs would be about $300,000 per year, and substantial progress should be clear in about five years. Much of the total development costs would and should come from the microform industry.

What about copyright? The system we have described depends utterly on the ability to make copies. Revision of the present copyright law is now before Congress, and it is vital to avoid prohibiting the flow of information for research by the wrong laws.

INTERACTIONS BETWEEN LIBRARIES AND SPECIAL-PURPOSE LIBRARIES

The most important changes in libraries will be (1) increasing interactions between libraries which will reduce duplication of holdings and (2) the growth of special purpose collections dealing in depth with narrow fields. Effective interaction will be greatly facilitated through some of the automation procedures which we are discussing.

Any interaction first requires some means for one library to know what is in the collection of another. Since it would be costly for one library to purchase and hold the individual catalogs of many other libraries, the best solution is a union catalog.

The appeal of a union catalog has long been felt, and indeed the National Union Catalog is a notable response. In its card form at the Library of Congress it of course suffers from the lack of accessibility to the country's other research centers. The published form will be widely available, and its cost, between $8,000 and $9,000 will not be prohibitive. But it will be far from complete, it will take ten years to print its 600 volumes, and those volumes can never be changed.[11]

A machine-readable union catalog can be kept up-to-date, and it can be structured in several ways in contrast to the National Union Catalog which is an author catalog only.

How can a machine-readable national union catalog be constructed? The card form of the National Union Catalog could

[11] It should be added that provision has been made for changing the "printer's copy" of the National Union Catalog during the course of publication from cards to machine-produced output at any time when this becomes practicable.

be key punched, but we think it preferable to grow the catalog by merging the machine-readable catalogs as they are developed by existing individual libraries. A union of several machine-readable catalogs (say, up to ten) could be constructed (see the Appendix to this chapter for details) at a cost of $12 for each reel of the union catalog, plus the cost of the tape. Unions of union catalogs would soon follow. We are assuming here that most of the decisions about whether two cards represent the same document can be made by a sophisticated computer program, so that expert human handling of the remaining difficult cases would not be unduly burdensome.

Since the union would include only the machine-readable portions of each library's catalog, it would initially omit substantial parts of the library's holdings. However, within a few years the union catalog would include all recent acquisitions and all books in common use. Such a catalog would serve the clientele of a medical or science library where the value of a book diminishes rapidly. It would be less useful in the general research library or to the scholar who requires seasoned material that is infrequently called for. For this reason it may be desirable when financially possible to supplement the current union catalogs with the National Union Catalog in machine-readable form.

Typically the catalog holdings of a moderate-sized library would include its own catalog, a union catalog, and perhaps a number of special purpose catalogs. The dividing line between special-purpose catalogs and indices will be very thin—one will blend into the other. By purchasing microfilm catalogs, the small library without a computer will obtain many of the advantages of machine-readable catalogs.

Unfortunately, access to a catalog is not the same as access to a collection, and there are limits to interlibrary lending in view of the prior claims of the local clientele. But photocopying has greatly broadened the possibility of sharing, particularly in the case of technical reports and journal articles; and most copying of this sort falls under the cover of fair use. In cases of urgent need, a facsimile could be made within minutes, but the price would be much higher.

The publication of union catalogs in machine-readable form will stimulate strong pressures for uniformity of bibliographic reference. This is most desirable, particularly if it can be extended to foreign documents.

Many of the special libraries will be national libraries, devoted to particular subject areas. Each will strive for completeness in its own area and will develop its own indexing system for that area. The subject areas will overlap very substantially, and their subject-indexing systems will reflect fundamentally different world views in the regions of overlap.

Special-purpose libraries should be very broadly defined. Thus, for example, the abstracts and indexes published by the Americal Chemical Society in many cases will be referred to for the same purposes as catalogs of other libraries.

Small new areas of knowledge have the great advantage that they can start a fresh body of information. Early progress in machine-readable text, machine retrieval of facts, and sophisticated machine searching will likely come in these areas, where computers will provide access to highly refined bodies of information.

Handbooks of facts, formulas, and algorithms will be created and used. Here innovation is properly left to experts within the special fields. The continuing function of libraries will be to make their results generally and uniformly available. An exception to this statement might be made in the case of a research library with staff librarians who were themselves scholars and whose collaboration in such projects would be highly valuable.

RECOMMENDATIONS

Recommendations must be weighed both with respect to their importance and the certainty that they can be achieved. Accordingly, we will start with the most important and sure possibilities.

The best hope for dealing with the increasing amount of material with which research libraries must cope is greatly to reduce multiple holdings of the same document in different libraries. This can be achieved by effective interactions between libraries; both existing libraries and special libraries which may be uniquely structured to handle "remote" business.

The key to such interactions is the machine-readable and, hence, reproducible catalog. With existing technology it is both possible and economical to keep catalogs of large libraries on many reels of magnetic computer tapes. These tape catalogs can be copied. They can be published via a computer-to-microfilm printer. They can be combined into union catalogs, searched to create subcatalogs, and restructured to facilitate different modes of referencing. They can be edited, corrected, and kept current. Thus any library can be accurately and currently informed on the holdings of a wide range of other institutions. Its users will be able to identify and order documents from other institutions.

Development of machine-readable catalogs, particularly union catalogs, is by far the most important and most certain recommendation which we can make. In addition, library interactions will be furthered by better copying facilities and microforms. The nature of these innovations is not as clear to us, despite the many possibilities which exist in the area of microforms. The major uncertainties arise from user acceptance and from copyright laws. Hence, a more timid and speculative development program must be undertaken here.

We have said nothing about communications. With adequate machine-readable catalogs, a workable network of library interactions can be based on existing facilities: the mails, the teletype, and the telephone. These links are a good starting point. Needless to say, interactions will be improved by the better channels that will be developed. However, the cost of networks is so great that libraries must share them with other users; it is not reasonable that libraries be prime movers in the development of new networks.

It is clear that automation can and should be applied to handle the internal operations of large libraries. Current manual operations are barely workable in present-sized libraries and threaten chaos in the larger institutions of the future. Fortunately, many library tasks are ideally suited to computer organization; we have no doubt that it will be effective. Moreover, some of the records used in internal operations will be useful in making catalogs.

To achieve these general ends, we can make certain more specific suggestions that are grouped under the areas of microform technology and computer technology.

The microform technology had best be developed in industrial laboratories concerned with reproduction and photographic processes. Many places with great competence already exist. However, some central direction is necessary to establish standards and to see that problems unique to libraries are solved. The commercial value of microform equipment, as estimated by present market analysis, may be insufficient to support the development of the system we have outlined. But once the complete system is in operation, it will be the foundation of an entire new industry. The development will consist of a number of separate machines and microforms. Their value depends not on individual machines but on the over-all system. Central direction must make sure that a complete set of machines is created for making all the transformations which we have discussed, and central direction must see that the machines are compatible.

Computer technology for routine library functions and for a machine-readable catalog can best be developed in a large, existing, operating library. Only in this way can we guarantee that a useful system will be created and that the transition from existing manual procedures to automated procedures is viable. Funds for the development should be supplied outside the libraries normal operating budget. However, the costs must continually be appraised so that the final system makes economic sense for libraries.

A fertile institution in which to develop library automation would include not only a library but also a strong computer science department and a strong library school. The differing viewpoints and experiences of library users, computing specialists, and librarians must be reconciled and focused on the library's problems if these problems are to be solved.

Technology offers the librarian a variety of means by which his problems may be lightened or even solved with consequent improvement in the library's service to research. At the same time technology offers an evolutionary advance toward a national library system which will realize the ideal of equal, rapid access to the nation's research treasures.

APPENDIX

COSTS ASSOCIATED WITH THE MACHINE-READABLE CATALOG

In this appendix we shall assume a computing system with 12 tape drives operating at 90,000 characters per second and with a relatively slow memory of about 300,000 8-bit characters. On-line secondary storage is not required. (An IBM 360/40 with these characteristics would cost about $3 per minute during the prime shift, including operators and air conditioned space.)

We shall also assume that the catalog consists of 5 million cards of 300 characters each. These are stored on 80 reels of magnetic tape with 60,000 cards per reel. Thus each reel contains about 18 million characters. (We have assumed a 2400-foot reel packed at 800 characters per inch with a packing efficiency of about 80 percent. Since the cost of a reel is about $60, the total cost of the magnetic tape is about $5000.

Since a pass over one 2400-foot reel at a rate of 112 inches per second takes 4 minutes and costs about $12, a pass over the entire catalog would take about 5 hours and cost about $1000.

A union catalog is simply a merging of its constituent catalogs. We assume that most of the decisions about whether two cards represent the same document can be made by a sophisticated computer program, so that expert human handling of the remaining difficult cases would not be unduly burdensome. If the number of libraries in the union is less than ten (which we assume to be the maximum available merge ratio), then a single merge pass will suffice and the cost will be $12 for each reel of the union catalog.

To sort the catalog, we first sort each reel separately and then merge. The time required to sort a single reel is essentially four times the time required to read and write it; the cost would be about $48. In our example two merge passes would be required, each occupying 4 minutes per reel and costing $12 per reel. Thus the total time for sorting and merging would be 24 minutes per reel, and the total cost would be $72 per reel. For a much smaller catalog (less than ten reels), one merge pass would suffice, and the cost would be $60 per reel. For a larger catalog (more than 100 reels) three merge passes would be required, and the cost would be $84 per reel.

For microform publication, we have taken estimates for the Stromberg-Carlson 4060 microfilm printer. It has a font of about 100 characters including both upper- and lower-case roman letters. The font can be produced in four sizes at rates varying from 30,000 to 90,000 characters per second. Special characters not in the font can also be drawn directly from digital descriptions of their shape. Thus the machine can accommodate the odd symbols which occasionally occur and can accommodate foreign alphabets. Assuming a speed of 50,000 characters per second, about 10 hours of printer time would be required to make a microfilm copy of the catalog.

Assuming 200 card images per foot of 16mm microfilm, about 30,000 feet are needed for the catalog. This presents material at about a 20 : 1 reduction. At $5 per hundred feet cost for processed microfilm, the film cost is $1500.

For a paper copy, we assumed a density of 40 cards per page and a reproduction cost of 3 cents per page.

These estimates can easily be incorrect by a factor of 2. We doubt that more accurate predictions are possible.

Charles Blitzer

Director, Office of Education and Training
Smithsonian Institution

Reuben Clark

Attorney, Wilmer, Cutler and Pickering

IV

Research Libraries and The Federal Government

America's research libraries and archives are a precious and irreplaceable national resource. Their collections, buildings, equipment, and trained staffs, which represent a public and private investment of untold millions of dollars, are indispensable to the pursuit of scholarship and research in the humanities and the social and physical sciences. They serve industry and government as well as the world of learning. They are truly the foundation upon which the edifice of knowledge is built.

Historically, America's research libraries, archives, and manuscript collections were created and have been since supported largely by private and state institutions, chiefly universities and research establishments of all kinds. Originally they were intended primarily to serve the faculties, students, and staffs of these institutions. They are now, however, also national institutions in a very real sense and undergird the entire national research effort. A government that has recognized the importance of basic research, and has accepted responsibility for supporting it, cannot afford to ignore the needs of research libraries and the opportunities inherent in the meeting of that need.

Today, demands upon America's research libraries and archives outrun their traditional sources of support. The accelerated pace of research in all disciplines, the opening up of new fields of knowledge, the vastly increased quantity of all types of publications throughout the world, and the sheer increase of the cost of books and other materials have confronted research libraries with staggering financial burdens. So, too, has the vastly expanded national effort in graduate and postdoctoral education. The ever-increasing complexity of the materials that scholars need requires of librarians new language and subject matter skills. Libraries are called upon to bear the cost of new types of sophisticated equipment that will permit them to fulfill their obligations more effectively. Above all, the pressing need to incorporate existing research libraries into a national system for the dissemination of information as to the location of materials and for providing access to them is clearly beyond the resources of the nation's research libraries themselves.

If the present situation of research libraries argues for increased Federal support, it also suggests some things about the form which such support should take. If research libraries are to be supported not as adjuncts to particular institutions but as crucially important, integrated national resources, then this support must be provided in ways calculated to make these resources as widely and easily available as possible. The establishment of a rational, coherent Federal program of support to research libraries offers a great opportunity to move toward the creation of a truly national system of research libraries.

The research libraries themselves have shown a laudable willingness to cooperate in order to meet the needs of the nation, notwithstanding the inherent difficulties that must arise when diverse, independent institutions seek to meet national requirements. Through such undertakings as the Farmington Plan, the Center for Research Libraries, the National Union Catalog, the Association of Research Libraries, and a number of less formal arrangements, such as the distribution of Library of Congress catalog cards, the country's research libraries have attempted, within limits set by available funds, to work toward the creation of a comprehensive library system in which ideally the resources of each library can be made more easily accessible to scholars, wherever located, and in which costly duplication of services and materials can be significantly reduced. It is now apparent that only with substantial Federal support and guidance can we hope for the realization of this goal.

Through such a system, every book would be cataloged only once, either by The National Library or by another research library nationally funded, and the result would be made rapidly available to every research library. Through such a system, every physically endangered book would be preserved, with micro- or photocopies being made available on demand to all libraries through Federal support.

Through such a system, research and development in library technology would be performed, both by The National Library and by other libraries nationally funded, and the result made available to all libraries.

The beneficiaries of a national library system would include all scholars and scientists, all educational institutions, all libraries, industry and government itself—indeed, all those in need of research materials. The Library of Congress, already the beneficiary of wise counsel and substantial appropriations from the Congress, has contributed signally to the beginnings of such a system. Partial systems have already been created in agriculture and medicine, through the National Agricultural Library and the National Library of Medicine. Such precedents should be extended to all other fields, building upon the great resources that now exist. The active and enlightened participation of the Federal government, dealing directly with the research libraries themselves, is required for the success of this enterprise.

A Federal program for research libraries, then, should serve two major purposes: (1) the support of research libraries themselves and, hence, of all research and scholarship and (2) the creation of a coherent national system of research libraries, minimizing unnecessary duplication, fostering cooperative efforts, and ensuring the freest possible access, consistent with local needs, to the resources of all libraries and archives embraced by the system. A Federal contribution, modest in comparison both with the vast sums already invested in America's research libraries and with the current scale of private contributions being made to their support, can serve, in effect, to "nationalize" this precious resource by making the collections of our research libraries accessible to scholars across the nation.[12]

Specifically, research libraries and their far-flung constituencies look to the Federal government for assistance of three related sorts. The first is direct financial support to research libraries. The second is a vigorous national library able and willing to undertake, starting within the limits of existing technology, a broad range of programs of research and service to the entire community of research libraries and those they serve. The third is the effective articulation and implementation of national policies and plans for research libraries, particularly taking into account the fact of rapid technological change in the areas of communication and information storage, location and retrieval. Of these, only the third entails a new departure for the Federal government; the other two already exist in embryonic form.

Research libraries currently receive, or are eligible to receive, Federal funds under a number of programs administered by a number of agencies and bureaus. Notwithstanding the current substantial level of support for research libraries, Federal funding is, in terms of need, grossly inadequate. In

[12] The extremely uneven geographical distribution of the nation's research libraries is a result of historical accident rather than of design. The deliberate creation of one or more great new research libraries, in addition to support of existing ones, has been advocated as a corrective to the present uneven distribution. Such an undertaking would itself necessarily draw upon existing research library resources, without which it would be unthinkable.

addition, Federal activities in this area are presently fragmented and are generally associated (often at a low administrative level) with agencies whose primary missions lie elsewhere.

Similarly, the Library of Congress is in effect The National Library of the United States. As such it has for many years performed a wide range of services beneficial to the entire community of research libraries and those they serve. In the absence of an official mandate to perform such services, and in view of its formal designation as a legislative library, the Library of Congress has been unable to move forward boldly with programs of national service to all research libraries. In particular, it has been reluctant to seek, as part of its own appropriation, the funds necessary to enable it to serve as a true national library and has tended instead to rely upon funds from other Federal agencies and from private sources for this purpose.

Nevertheless, both in the case of direct financial support to research libraries and in the case of the Library of Congress, clear precedents have been established upon which a truly comprehensive and effective Federal program can be built. What must be added is a coordinating and stimulating intelligence—a body that will be sensitive to the qualities and needs of research libraries and those they serve, that will take cognizance of all Federal programs affecting research libraries and that will serve as a force both of coordination and of innovation.

A single agency of the Federal government should be given responsibility and authority for all Federal programs directly related to research libraries. Since the Library of Congress (acting as a national library) will inevitably continue to play a major role in this sphere, such a solution would necessarily involve a change in its status.

Following the precedent of the National Museum Act of 1966, a National Library Act could transform the Library of Congress into a true national library. The new national library could then be explicitly authorized to continue and expand its programs of research and national service to research libraries, to receive both appropriated and private funds for the purpose of making grants to research libraries, and to bear major responsibility for the coordination of all Federal programs affecting libraries. Of course the Library of Congress must, in any event, continue to serve as the legislative library of the United States. To this end, its Legislative Reference Service (perhaps restyled the Legislative Research Service) should build upon its already impressive strength and expertness, guided by the Joint Congressional Committee on the Library of Congress. In performing its national services, the national library, which might be known as "The Library of Congress: The National Library of the United States," should be guided by a strong and distinguished Board of Trustees, composed of both public and private members. The Board of Regents of the Smithsonian Institution, which represents the private sector as well as the three branches of the Federal government, is a possible model for this Board.

Under this scheme, operating funds for the Legislative Reference Service would remain within the legislative section of the Federal budget. Funds for national programs, whether performed directly by the national library or by grants to other libraries, could be appropriated to the Library of Congress in the executive branch section of the Federal budget, either as an appropriation to an independent agency or under the category of Appropriations to the President of the United States.

Ideally, "The Library of Congress: The National Library" would embrace the existing National Library of Medicine and the National Agricultural Library. Failing this, every effort should be made to assure the greatest possible degree of cooperation among the three national libraries in order that duplication might be minimized and that cooperative efforts and compatible systems might be encouraged.

Such a structure, designed to associate as closely as possible national library services and Federal grants to research libraries, would offer the best assurance that Federal programs in this field would be carried on with the greatest possible efficiency and the most beneficial results. We are aware, however, that the location of the Library of Congress within the legislative branch of the Federal government, and its official status as a legislative library, pose serious questions as to the feasibility of moving immediately to a solution that combines in a single institution an operating national library and a program of Federal grants to libraries. Even so, certain steps can and should be taken now to improve the effectiveness of Federal programs relating to research libraries and to bring us closer to the realization of the ultimate goal. We propose, then, three immediate steps for better organizing in the national interest the three functions stated above: direct financial assistance, national library service, and planning and research.

First, we propose that there be created within the Department of Health, Education, and Welfare, and reporting to the Secretary, a permanent Commission on Libraries and Archives, the members to be appointed by the President of the United States. The members of this Commission should represent education, scholarship in the humanities, research in the natural and social sciences, the library and archival professions, and the public interest generally. Affected Federal agencies, including the Library of Congress, the National Archives, the National Agricultural Library, and the National Library of Medicine, should be required to send observers regularly to the Commission's meetings. The Commission should have a competent staff and adequate funds for long-range planning and research. The Commission should, among other functions, have continuing responsibility for advising the Federal government on national library needs, for assessing the continued efficacy of existing library legislation and the impact upon libraries of all Federal legislation, as well as the implications for libraries of technological change; it could serve also as an advisory board for the Library of Congress, the other national libraries, and the National Archives; and it should bear a special responsibility for advising the Secretary of Health, Education, and Welfare and the Commissioner of Education about library programs of the Department. The Commission should be required by law to report each year to the Congress and the President, making such recommendations as seem to it desirable concerning Federal activities affecting libraries and archives.

This Commission would provide an essential overview of all Federal library programs and legislation. Since our specific concern is with research libraries, we propose, second, that all present programs of the Office of Education affecting research libraries be brought together in a single Division within that Office. The administration of new Federal programs affecting research libraries should also be placed within this Division. This would mean, for example, that funds presently available for construction of research library facilities, training of research librarians, acquisition of materials and performing of bibliographical services, and research and development would all be administered by a single Division of Research Libraries and Archives. This Division, acting under the policy direction of the Commission, should have as its mission the improvement of research library and archival services throughout the nation. It should administer Federal grant programs in these areas, building upon existing resources, both public and private. It should be authorized explicitly to make grants to such public institutions as the Library of Congress, as well as to other public and private research libraries, for the performance of national library services, including acquisition, preservation, and dissemination of library materials, cataloging and other bibliographical services, and research and development aimed at technological improvement of library and archival services.

We would recommend to the Secretary of Health, Education, and Welfare and the Commissioner of Education that this Division of Research Libraries and Archives be placed within the Bureau of Higher Education of the United States

Office of Education. While we are aware of the arguments in favor of a consolidation of all library programs—public, school, college, and research—we are persuaded that the special character of research libraries and of those they serve makes the Bureau of Higher Education a more suitable location for programs affecting research libraries than the Bureau of Adult, Vocational and Library Programs or any other existing Bureau of the Office of Education. Furthermore, we believe that necessary coordination of all library programs can be accomplished through the efforts of the permanent Commission on Libraries and Archives.

Third, we propose that the Congress of the United States declare that the Library of Congress is, in addition to its role as legislative library, the National Library of the United States with responsibility and authority to undertake programs of acquisition, cataloging, preservation, dissemination, training, research and development, and to perform related services, either directly or by contract with other institutions, in the national interest.

Ralph S. Brown, Jr.
Simeon E. Baldwin Professor of Law
Yale Law School

Appendix

Copyright Problems of Research Libraries

This memorandum will concentrate on issues that have developed because of the availability of cheap and easy reproduction of all kinds of documents, either by reprography—a technique already well advanced—or by electronic storage and retrieval, the application of which to library collections may be imminent. Much of the copying that these technologies permit or require may call for clearance and payments in order to avoid copyright infringement. Clearance and payments, in the modern setting, are burdensome. What is to be done?

Some resolution of the differences between copyright owners and library users is bound to emerge from the general revision of the copyright law now pending in the Congress. A bill passed the House in April 1967. Prompt hearings in the Senate created a further opportunity to express opposition to parts of the bill that are claimed to be immoderately restrictive of reprographic copying and computer services. Such opposition had been relatively tardy in making itself heard, when one considers that draft bills have been circulating since 1961. But now the complaints have reached senatorial ears. The current result is a bill (S. 2216, introduced by Senator McClellan, Aug. 2, 1967) to create a "National

Commission on New Technological Uses of Copyrighted Works."

The bill's statement of purpose is close to the major copyright concerns of research libraries:

> The purpose of the Commission is to study and compile data on the reproduction and use of copyrighted works of authorship (1) in automatic systems capable of storing, processing, retrieving, and transferring information, and (2) by various forms of machine reproduction. The Commission shall make recommendations as to such changes in copyright law or procedures that may be necessary to assure for such purposes access to copyrighted works, and to provide recognition of the rights of copyright owners.

Whether such a commission will come into being, and, if it does, the consequences for the general revision effort, are at this writing wholly speculative. The issues abide.

REPROGRAPHY

The legal status of reprography (photocopying plus other copying methods that do not technically involve photographic processes) and of computer use differ somewhat, and should be separately summarized.

The extent of permissible copying of copyrighted documents, for scholarly purposes, is not a new problem. The concept of "fair use" of copyrighted materials has long been assumed to permit the hand copying of excerpts from copyrighted works by researchers. The arduous nature of manual copying tended to establish its own limits. If the researcher then, as an author, reproduced such excerpts in his own published work, with or without quotation or attribution, the notion of fair use again came into play. While its contours were vague, judicial definition, and agreements among publishers, such as the Resolution on Permissions of the Association of American University Presses, made the rules workable. The development of photocopying, from beginnings more than half a century ago, brushed aside the constraints of hand copying. For libraries that furnished or used photocopies, appropriate limits have never been firmly resolved, despite such efforts as the "Gentlemen's Agreement" of 1935 and subsequent attempts by the American Library Association to gain recognition for the practice of furnishing single copies to scholars either of parts of a work, or of the entire work (with certain qualifications relating to its availability). Libraries stated their position before the House Committee which shaped the present general revision bill. They all, I believe, favored wide leeway; some thought that there should be a statutory definition, others preferred the conclusion reached by the committee which, in its 1967 Report, said that it "does not favor a specific provision dealing with library photocopying." (H.R. Report No. 90 90th Cong. 1st Session, p. 36.)

Meanwhile, the photocopying flood was upon us. In libraries as well as in educational institutions generally, copying goes on that would not be legally permissible under conventional criteria of fair use. At the same time, some surveys that were made tended to show that the bulk of photocopying was from scholarly journals, and that, up to the present time, such copying served the cause of increased dissemination of research work (especially in the sciences), and did not appear to be causing serious economic harm to the journals from which copies were being made.

But even if the surveys accurately reflected the situation in the early 1960's, it was rapidly changing as reprographic methods became ever better and cheaper. By 1966, the ineffable Marshall McLuhan had already proclaimed that "In the age of Xerox, the reader becomes a publisher." Professor Marke comments on this dictum, "In essence, this is exactly what commercial publishers fear." And not only commercial publishers; university presses have a similar concern. How should the moderately elastic doctrine of fair use, or even the principle of copyright itself, adjust to the reprographic explosion, one of the many explosions of our time?

COMPUTERS

Any current problem that is not an explosion is a revolution. The potentialities of electronic storage and retrieval of information may indeed revolutionize publishing, libraries, and reading.

Copyright law has not yet taken on the computer. The Copyright Office is accepting computer programs (that is, instructions and systems for getting data in and out of computers) as copyrightable material; but that practice, of debatable propriety, has little significance until it is tested in the courts. For libraries, the recognition of exclusive rights in programs, whether by copyright or by patent, would be troublesome; but I doubt that much will come of this push for protection. In any event, I cannot deal with it in this paper.

The burning question is the status of computer inputs and outputs of copyrighted material, however they are programmed. Some legal conclusions can be baldly stated, with respect to the present state of the law, and the general revision in its current form.

1. A computer printout of a copyrighted text, or a substantial part of a text, is an infringing copy, unless it falls within the scope of fair use. There is no reason to think that fair use should be differently defined for computer "hard" copies, even though the computer is undiscriminating, tireless, and prolix. The revision bill does not alter this situation.

2. Suppose that a computer produces a rearrangement of significant parts of the copyrighted work (assuming that what is produced is from the "expression" of the author and not simply his "ideas" or "information," terms that also embrace a large set of issues). For example, it is directed to extract and rearrange all the references to marriage customs from a book on Polynesia. This will probably infringe the copyright owner's exclusive right to "translate the copyrighted

work into other languages or dialects, or make any other version thereof, if it be a literary work. . . ." "Literary" in this setting does not have any esthetic content; it is simply a way of distinguishing musical works, works of art, and so on. (Sec. 1(a); cf. Sec. 7). The general revision bill removes most definitional ambiguities by giving the author an exclusive right "to prepare derivative works based upon the copyrighted work," keyed to a generous definition of "derivative work," which embraces "any other form in which a work may be recast, transformed, or adapted." (Secs. 106, 101.) It has a marginally broader reach than the present law.

3. Suppose that a retrieval system, instead of making a printout, shows the whole or a significant portion of the work on a screen, either in the library, or in a researcher's office (for present purposes I am ignoring the more difficult questions of classroom and other like displays). Under the present law, this is probably not an infringement. The act does not address itself specifically to transitory displays, only to exhibits or representations, which may not be the same thing. It could be argued that a projection is just a reading aid; it is the usual way of reading microfilm. But if the retrieval input had not been authorized, a court sympathetic to authors could declare that the display infringed, as a kind of ephemeral copying.

The revision bill is again clarifying, in that the copyright owner would indeed have the exclusive right "to display the copyrighted work publicly"[13] (Sec. 106). "Display" is adequately defined. Discussion about the new display right has centered more on classroom and other student use of teaching materials than on the needs of research libraries. Discrimination is called for, to avoid any unintended restraints on transiently showing parts of the work, as a research scanning technique, like leafing through a book.

[13] No comfort should be sought from the word, "publicly." As defined (Sec. 101), it would cover an on-demand scanning device. See H.R. Rep. No. 83, 90th Cong. 1st Sess. 28–29, 31 (1967).

Practically, ephemeral projections from photocopies and from computers should be treated alike, with considerable scope for fair use, and a library privilege of display to readers if the work displayed is legitimately in the possession of the library. Sec. 109(b) of the House bill comes close to meeting this need. It exempts a display to "viewers present at the place where the copy is located."[14]

4. This brings us to the status of computer inputs for storage (what is functionally first I have intentionally put last in this summary, because it involves the sharpest controversy). In my opinion, under the present law input and storage, without more, are not infringement. Conventionally, to copy a visually perceptible work requires the production of a visually perceptible equivalent. A 1952 amendment to the statute did prohibit the making of "any transcription or record" of a copyrighted work from which it could "by any method be exhibited, delivered, presented, produced, or reproduced" (Sec. 1(c)). But it is doubtful that this language, which is in a passage directed to the *oral* presentation of copyrighted work *for profit,* intended to cover the invisible electrical imprints inside a computer.[15]

Whatever the uncertainties of present law, there is little question that the House bill intends to make input a form of copying. This results from the otherwise commendable departure in the new bill from the old requirement that a

[14] Does the "place where" include the Widener Library? The Harvard campus? A faculty member's "on-line" study in Lexington? Probably only the first; see H.R. Rep. No. 83, p. 39. This seems unduly confining. This point is influenced by the disputes about radio and TV transmissions, and other classroom displays, which are very complicated. *Ibid.* 40–46.

[15] It is also argued, I believe, that putting a written work into machine-readable form necessarily requires making a "version" of it. This is an ingenious contention, but it probably fails if the process results only in operations that are not visually readable. Thus, the distorted numbers on a bank check are readable, but card-punches or magnetic impressions are not.

copy be tangible and intelligible. The revision bill defines a copy as a "material object" (for example, a magnetic tape) "from which the work can be perceived, reproduced, or otherwise communicated, either directly or with the aid of a machine or device" (Sec. 101).

The interesting question is not what is proposed, but why. Although there has been little sustained discussion, copyright spokesmen are insistent that computer input should be controlled; computer spokesmen are equally insistent that it should not be. Why do publishers want to control what goes into the storage system, if they can control what comes out? The answer lies partly in the "if." Publishers argue that they will not be able to police the output of computerized systems, just as they fear the present proliferation of photocopying machines. A partial rejoinder to this fear is that you cannot hide a complex storage and retrieval system in a closet. Further, it is hard to imagine how a price could be set on inputs, unless both parties had a fairly clear idea what use was to be made of the stored work. To be sure, some value could be attached to the availability of the work in the system. This raises the possibility that copyright owners hope to exact a charge for what would otherwise be fair use of the work, for example, to search it for particular ideas or bits of data that would ordinarily be open to use without permission.

One may also speculate that publishers, faced with the great unknown of the effect of future systems on the market for conventional printed works, want to get control of the use of their works in the new technology at the earliest possible stage. By the same token, those who are engaged in fashioning the brave new world want to be free of such controls until they produce copies or displays that would fall within the scope of copyright as hitherto understood. And perhaps they want to have even greater freedom. This leads to consideration of the emerging clash of attitudes about copyright.

OPPOSED POSITIONS

Behind the skirmish lines, sniping away from one outpost or another, two main bodies of opinion may be forming. The martial analogy is closer to Vietnam than to Waterloo, but two main-force positions can be identified amidst the swirl of debate.

1. One position (I state it in extreme terms) views copyright as an obstruction on the path of progress. It may be a manageable system for recognizing rights in the entertainment industries, but it should not be permitted to slow down the magnificent advance of science, education, and research libraries. Research libraries, we are told, exist to facilitate copying. They now have within their reach devices for finding and transmitting knowledge (by way of copies of documents) that are quite incompatible with the clumsy necessities of identifying a copyright holder and obtaining his permission. The cost of the permission, and even more the cost of obtaining it and the time it takes, threaten to block the free flow of information. Therefore, copyright is obsolescent. The producers of knowledge have other sources of support anyhow. To the extent that a replacement for the rewards of copyright is needed, let the government subsidize authorship as it is subsidizing education. We observe this happening on a large scale, first in natural science and now in educational research itself. The policy of the Office of Education, not to permit copyright in works supported by it, is the right one, and should be extended.

If it is granted that this position cannot prevail, owing to the obstinate resistance of authors and publishers, then the system will be tolerable only if the publishers organize a system of clearances that will keep the use of copyrighted materials in reprography and computers cheap and easy.

2. The contrary view, standing on hard-won and long-held high ground, sees copyright as a minimal expression of the natural right of an author to deal as he will with his own

intellectual creation. It is a right that has constitutional recognition. A reasonable statutory framework permits creative authors through their agents, usually publishers, to control any reproduction of their work. A wise policy permits the free use of ideas; but the author's expression, mixed as it is with his labor, is his to exploit. Those who want copies must pay for them, just as they do for the hardware they use to make the copies.

As a concession, if the volume and variety of desired copying make it difficult to seek out the author, then it is up to the users to develop a scheme that will keep copying easy. Since they are probably destroying the normal sources of income for the author, there is not reason for users to expect that their machine copying will be cheap.

It soon becomes apparent, when one attempts to use either of these polar positions as a basis for action, that neither can be uniformly applicable. That part of the copyright world which is of special concern to research libraries is only one of several continents. And within that continent there are subareas where varying considerations apply. I will give only two examples.

One is the status of scientific papers, ordinarily published in one of the thousands of specialized journals. There has been much talk and even some investigation of the hindrance of copyright to extensive machine copying. Assertions that authors of scientific papers have no expectations of commercial exploitation through copyright seem altogether plausible. If there is no strong copyright interest, there is a fairly simple solution. Instead of pushing legal measures to make copyright ineffective, why shouldn't we persuade scientific authors not to claim copyright? Fortunately, an effort to make copyright automatic (without any claim by notice or registration) has had no success in the revision efforts. While it is easy to get copyright, it is just as easy to put one's work in the public domain.

Librarians might well consider launching a campaign for

abstention from copyright, or for limited copyright, in scholarly publications. An example of what I call "limited copyright" comes, appropriately enough, from a useful recent symposium on Reprography and Copyright Law. It reads as follows:

Copyright, 1964, By George P. Bush

George P. Bush will not enforce his copyright after January 1, 1970. Permission to copy the whole or part of this document is hereby granted to those who wish to use such copies in educational works, professional journals, as well as in an information handling storage or retrieval system. Permission to others to copy is governed by "Fair Use."

This sort of limited claim to copyright could, through the efforts of librarians and others, be codified in two or three standard categories. These could then be identified by simple symbols. This is not the place to develop such a scheme; but it does illustrate that copyright need not be an all-or-nothing affair.

One difficulty with the abandonment of copyright is the lack of other adequate legal controls against fraudulent copying (taking and misrepresenting another's work as one's own), and the similarly imperfect state of the law in respect to assigning proper credit when avowedly borrowing the work of others (one aspect of the notions embraced in "moral right"). If the statutory system were not so obsessed with perfecting and tightening copyright, it would pay more attention to these intermediate kinds of protection. But there is some possibility of achieving them through voluntary action, if there does exist the claimed consensus within the scientific community about the free dissemination of scientific papers (a consensus, one might observe, that surely does not obtain with respect to texts and other works that can earn royalties).

What has just been said ignores the economics of journal publishing. Many journals are entirely supported by subscriptions, most of which come from libraries. Others are partly subsidized by sponsoring societies, and so forth. While it may be that so far machine copying has led to no decline in subscription revenues, when one looks farther ahead great changes are in prospect. The visions of an "on-demand" reproduction system can carry one to the point where only one copy of a work need be acquired for a regional system comprehending scores of libraries as we now know them. Looking even farther ahead, we are asked to consider why even one copy, in any conventional format, is necessary. The thoughts of an author may be composed directly onto microfilm or magnetic tape (exposing us all to the unedited outpourings of ubiquitous dictating units!).

As we approach these transformations, the whole institution of publishing will have to be reconstructed, and copyright along with it.

If scientific journals may be an example of a consensual solution, my second example clearly is not. Briefly, it concerns the Educational Research Information Center of the Office of Education. ERIC has doubtless laudable aims. But (this is from a partisan account, a publisher's), ERIC has been seeking, without offering compensation, blanket permissions to microfilm quantities of educational titles that are commercially published. If the publishers are cold to these requests, they may not be unreasonably so. The magic words "education," "research," and "microfilm" are no substitute for sales of the books. If ERIC is going to distribute 50 copies to state Boards of Education, why doesn't it buy 50 copies?

This episode is incomplete. By now some accommodation may have been found, so one should withhold final judgment. It does seem to represent a fairly clear collision of interests. It could be resolved by legislation; it might be more easily resolved by compensation, that is by simply paying for what is taken.

CLEARINGHOUSE PROPOSALS

A discussion of compensation for machine reproduction leads quickly to consideration of general licensing arrangements. Some kind of central clearinghouse is variously seen as a panacea, or as a monstrosity that, in one publisher's words, "spends dollars to collect dimes."

Licensing and clearing arrangements need much more detailed examination than they have so far received. We already have long-standing and elaborate arrangements for the licensing of public performance of copyrighted music, through ASCAP and other performing-rights organizations. These will serve as a guide but not as a model. ASCAP deals with something transient, a performance, but detectability is made less difficult because it is only *public* performances for profit that are to be licensed. The bulk of ASCAP's revenues come from a few large users, the broadcasting networks; large computer networks may turn out to be similarly visible. ASCAP also tries to police a tangled fringe of small users; this experience has some bearing on the photocopying market.

At this stage, however, we have no data on which to begin to construct charges for blanket licensing of an entire repertory, as ASCAP does. A blanket license still requires a way to meter copying, either totally or through a good sample, in order to provide a basis for distribution among the copyright holders. It is the prospect of recording and reporting copying of all shapes and sizes that stimulates fears of costly obstructions to rational retrieval systems. Is it thinkable that the ingenuity that can produce computer systems cannot build into them copyright metering devices? A copyright reference can permeate a computer input just as thoroughly as does the identity of the work. In reprography of parts of a copyrighted document, identification of copyright claims may be more difficult. Still, microcopying must be similar to computer storage, in that the identity of the work presumably appears on each card or microfiche. Copyright data can go along with it.

Casual photocopying on the office Xerox may not be controllable. The proposal for a licensing scheme in which payment would be made through adhesive stamps seems curiously archaic in an electronic age.

Another major aspect of centralized licensing that has not been adequately explored is the probable need for some degree of public regulation. Again the ASCAP and BMI experience is illustrative. When you have a massive pooling of copyrights on the publishers' side, even if (indeed, especially if) the publishers are confronted with an alliance of users, the antitrust laws cannot be ignored. ASCAP, and to a lesser extent BMI, have been subject to regulation of their rates and practices since 1941. It is a curious form of regulation, with the Antitrust Division of the Department of Justice as the watchdog, and the Federal courts as sometimes ill-equipped enforcers. Antitrust consent decrees are the source of standards for regulation. There are no statutory criteria at all, except the underlying sanctions of the antitrust laws, which are intended to maintain competition, not to regulate monopolies.

WHERE NEXT?

For research libraries, as they rethink their mission and calculate the resources needed for it, the new technologies loom large. They are going to be costly, and anything that adds to their cost is understandably disfavored. Clearing and paying for copyright permissions are so stigmatized.

It seems to me that compensation for authors and publishers, now underwritten by the institution of copyright, is not properly viewed as a parasitic charge. It has always been part of the cost of maintaining libraries in modern times, as part of the price of the book. To the extent that the new technologies make some of the functions of publishers redundant, for example the manufacture and distribution of books, publishers have no claim to continued payments. They will have to see if they can compete in the manufacture and distribution of microfiches and tapes. But machine authorship and editing are beyond present horizons. Those are the creative and ordering functions that have to be supported somehow. Increasing, preserving, and diffusing knowledge all have their costs that have to be faced and somehow fairly apportioned.

Legislative action can and does powerfully affect these apportionments. Thus, the present law, by protecting public performances of music and other nondramatic works only when they are "for profit," creates a sector of free use for educational institutions (but there is not and never has been a blanket exemption for nonprofit users). In the current enterprise, there is considerable and justified irritation with the copyright interests, who appear to be chiefly concerned with enlarging their rights, and to be giving very little constructive thought to the new era. (On their part, they complain that educational users particularly are simply demanding exemptions that cut down copyright, and likewise are not seeking ways of accommodation.) When one looks again at the copyright revision proposals, the impression does emerge that there is a lot in them for the authors and publishers and not much for the consumer. The substantial extension in duration of copyrights (on the average, 50 percent) is the most conspicuous example.

But such irritants (or worse) should not obscure what seems to me the main consideration. The new technologies, with their speed and abundance, raise formidable challenges of convenience and efficiency to the copyright system. The costs of clearance, that is obtaining information about claims to copyright, must be brought down, and the costs of using copyright works bargained out. That is where the main effort is needed. I should, however, reiterate that these exhortations are not intended to imply that the legal posture is unimportant. Clearly, one interest or another can be powerfully preferred by the grant or denial of legal rights. The present program should be to move on with most of the revision enterprise (which, on technical grounds, is sorely needed). The Congress, in the troubled fields here reviewed, must for a while attempt the difficult feat of standing still on a tightrope.

SELECTED REFERENCES

The first two items collect useful data on the problems here discussed:

1. L. Hattery and G. Bush, *Reprography and Copyright Law,* 1964 (papers from a 1963 symposium at American University).
2. J. Marke, *Copyright and Intellectual Property.* Fund for the Advancement of Education, 1967, esp. pp. 72–105.
3. U.S. House of Rep. Comm. on the Judiciary, H.R. Rep. No. 83, *Copyright Law Revision,* March 8, 1967.
4. American Council of Learned Societies, *Revision of the Copyright Law,* ACLS Newsletter, Dec. 1965, p. 1.
5. Interuniversity Communications Council (EDUCOM), *The Copyright Revision Bill in Relation to Computers,* March 1967.
6. C. Benjamin, *Computers, Copyrights and Educators,* address June 19, 1967 (ERIC episode).

Index

American Council of Learned Societies–Committee on Research Libraries
members of, vii–viii
Preface, ix–x
recommendations, 1–25
American Library Association, arrangements for publishing the National Union Catalog completed by, 34
Association of Research Libraries
membership of, xiii–xiv
plan to preserve and film "brittle" books, 10
program of resource development deserving of support, 14, 46
statement to the National Advisory Commission on Libraries, 23
Automation, *see* Computer in library operations, Library technology, Microreproduction

Baker, William O., vii
Barrow, William J., researches on book papers, 16–17
Beasley, Kenneth E., Committee debt to acknowledged, 19n
Bibliography
adequacy of questioned, xv, 29
bibliographical services of the Library of Congress, 7–8, 28–38 *passim*
Committee recommendation to establish National Bibliographical Office, 6–8
case for, 30
functions of, 8–9
Blitzer, Charles, 77
Book papers
Committee recommendation for adoption of lasting book papers, 16–17
further research needed, 48–49
impermanence of, xvi, 16, 47
plan for the preservation of deteriorating books, 10, 47–48
Brewster, Kingman, Jr., vii
Brockway, Thomas P., viii
Broughton, T. Robert S., vii
Brown, Ralph S., 86
Brown, W. Stanley, 59
Bryant, Douglas W., vii
Burkhardt, Frederick, v, vii
Butterfield, Lyman H., vii

Cataloging, *see* Library cataloging *and* Computer in library operations
Center for Research Libraries
 incorporation in national library system
 as national depository and lending library, 12–13, 50–52
 recommended by Committee, 12–13
Clapp, Verner W.
 Council support of library research during his presidency, 19
 thanked for Council on Library Resources grant, v
Clark, Reuben, 77
Commission, a National Library, *see* Library Commission
Committee on Research Libraries, *see* American Council of Learned Societies–Committee on Research Libraries
Computer in library operations
 cataloging, 35–37, 60–65
 construction of machine-readable catalogs, 65–66
 costs, 37, 63–64, 75–76
 development of computer technology, 74–75
 experiments in, 31, 36–37
 library functions other than cataloging, 65–66, 74
 licensing of machine reproduction, 96–98
 problems of copyright, 89–92
 promise and limitations in, xvii
Copyright
 bearing on reprography and computer programs, 87–93
 bibliography, 100
 Committee recommendation on, 15–16
 extreme positions stated, 93–94
 limited copyright proposed, 94–95
 possibility in a clearinghouse, 96–98
 revision of present law, 98–99
Council on Library Resources
 as example of foundation support of library research, 19
 financing of research on book papers, 16
 thanked for grant for Research Libray Committee study,

Dix, William S., vii

Education, Office of, proposal to combine programs affecting research libraries in single Office of Education Division, 3, 84–85
 See also ERIC
Electronic storage and retrieval, *see* Computer in library operations
ERIC (Educational Research Information Center) of the Office of Education, example of, 31–32

Fair use, doctrine of, as affected by new technology, 15, 87–88
Farmington Plan
 aim of perhaps otherwise realized, 13–14, 40
 example of specialization in library acquisition, 50
 importance of its committees, 13–14
Federal support of research libraries, nature and necessity of, 2, 22–25, 80–81, 82–84
Ford Foundation
 establishment of Council on Library Resources by, 19
 grant to Association of Research Libraries to develop materials on Mainland China, 14, 46
Foundations as source of research library support, 18–19
Fussler, Herman H., vii

Haas, Warren J., vii
Harris, Chauncy D., vii
Hart, James D., vii
Harvard University, mounting library costs at, 44–45
Haviland, H. Field, Jr., viii
Health, Education, and Welfare, Department of, as suitable location for permanent National Library Commission, 3, 83–84
Higher Education Act of 1965
  amendment relating to Center for Research Libraries, 5, 13
  other changes proposed, 23–24
  provisions in relating to research materials, 5, 32–34

Information storage and retrieval, *see* Computer in library operations
INTREX, Massachusetts Institute of Technology experiment with computer-based engineering library, 36–37

Librarians
  shortage of, xvi
  training, 24
Libraries, historical society, support of, 22
Library, research, *see* Research libraries
Library acquisition
  Committee recommendation on, 4–6
  sharing of resources, 49–52
  substitutes for books, 46–47
  survey of problems, 41–45
Library cataloging
  arrearages in, xv
  survey of, 32–39
  see also Computer in library operations
Library Commission
  establishment of recommended, 2–4, 83–84
  functions of, 4–11, 84
Library of Congress
  acquisition of research materials by, 4–6
  bibliographical services performed, 7–8, 32–36
  Committee recommendation to designate Library of Congress as The National Library, 11–12, 81–83, 85
  project MARC, 9
Library cooperation
  extent and examples of, 2, 43, 47, 48, 52, 78–79
  facilitated by machine-readable catalogs, 70–72
  see also National Library System
Library networks, *see* National Library System
Library technology
  development of, responsibility of proposed Library Commission, 9–11
  evolutionary approach recommended, 55, 59–60
  promise and risks, xvii
  scientific libraries demonstrate possibilities in, 56
  see also Computer in library operations *and* Microreproduction

Machine-readable library data, *see* Computer in library operations
MARC, Library of Congress experiment with machine-readable cataloging data, 9
Mathews, Max V., 59
Medical Library Assistance Act of 1965 as example of enlightened Federal support, 56
MEDLARS, electronic storage and retrieval of medical data, 31
Microfilm, *see* Microreproduction
Microform, *see* Microreproduction

Microreproduction
  coordination of, needed, 8
  development of microform technology, 69–70, 74
  effect on journal publishing, 95–96
  importance of, 10, 66
  increasing reliance on, 46–47, 53–54
  requirements for an integrated system, 67–69
  why adoption slow, 67

National Bibliographical Office, *see* Bibliography
National Library Commission, *see* Library Commission
National Library System
  described and advocated, 78–80
  as objective, 1, 25
National Union Catalog (NUC)
  advantage of machine-readable union catalogs, 8, 35–37
  advantage of publication in book form, 34–35
  construction of machine-readable union catalogs by stages, 70–72
National Union Catalog of Manuscript Collections, Federal support for recommended, 8
Networks, library. *See* National Library System

Paper, permanent/durable, *see* Book papers
Photocopying, *see* Reprography
Public Law 480
  acquisitions under, 42
  continuance and extension of recommended, 5, 6

Ray, Gordon N., viii
Reprography
  effect on journal publishing, 95–96
  legal status of, 87–88
  public regulation of, 98
  see also Microreproduction
Research libraries, Federal program for proposed, 83–85
  importance of, xiii–xiv, 26
  mounting demands on, 26–28, 78
  problems of, ix, xiv–xviii
  support of, private and public, recommended, 18–25

United States Book Exchange, support of advocated, 25, 43

Vosper, Robert G., viii

Wells, Herman B, viii
Whitehill, Walter Muir, viii
Williams, Edwin E., 26
Williams, Gordon R., viii
Wolf, Edwin, 2nd, viii
Wright, Louis B., viii